The
THOUGHTFUL
LEADER

Mindy Gibbins-Klein is founder and director of REAL Thought Leaders, The Book Midwife® and Panoma Press business publishing. A Fellow of the Professional Speaking Association of the UK and Ireland, Mindy is a highly sought after speaker to executive audiences; she also develops and presents workshops and training programs for top business leaders. She has spoken to thousands of people in many countries around the world. Mindy is a regular columnist for several magazines and online publications such as the Huffington Post.

The
THOUGHTFUL LEADER

How to Use Your Head and
Your Heart to Inspire Others

MINDY GIBBINS-KLEIN

Published by
Rupa Publications India Pvt. Ltd 2025
7/16, Ansari Road, Daryaganj
New Delhi 110002

Sales centres:
Bengaluru Chennai
Hyderabad Jaipur Kathmandu
Kolkata Mumbai Prayagraj

Copyright © Mindy Gibbins-Klein 2025
This edition of The Thoughtful Leader: How to Use Your Head and Your Heart to Inspire Others is published by arrangement with Rethink Press.

The views and opinions expressed in this book are the author's own and the facts are as reported by her which have been verified to the extent possible, and the publishers are not in any way liable for the same.

All rights reserved.
No part of this publication may be reproduced, transmitted, or stored in a retrieval system, in any form or by any means, electronic, mechanical, photocopying, recording or otherwise, without the prior permission of the publisher.

P-ISBN: 978-93-5702-775-5
E-ISBN: 978-93-5702-699-4

First impression 2025

10 9 8 7 6 5 4 3 2 1

The moral right of the author has been asserted.

Printed in India

This book is sold subject to the condition that it shall not, by way of trade or otherwise, be lent, resold, hired out, or otherwise circulated, without the publisher's prior consent, in any form of binding or cover other than that in which it is published.

Dedication and Acknowledgements

This book is dedicated to the many talented and generous mentors who have guided me on my path, and to the many clients, colleagues and friends I've made along that path.

Thank you so much to the following people for all the help, support, encouragement, inspiration, friendship, and patience. It's not an exhaustive list, and I'm sure I've forgotten important people, in which case I'll be groveling and making it up to you. I've made this list alphabetical so there's no need to read too much into the order!

- Dawattie Basdeo
- Alison Baugh
- Tim Bean
- Dan Bradbury
- Rob Brown
- Neil Coe
- Jenny Garrett
- Bradley Gibbins-Klein
- Taz Gibbins-Klein
- Phil Gibbins-Klein
- Seth Godin
- Andi Grant Edwards
- Emma Herbert
- Philippa Hull
- Kate Keenan
- Tiffany Kemp
- Sandi Klein
- Gail Maisel
- Rob Maisel
- Karen Mena
- Chris Merrington
- Penny Power
- Thomas Power
- Daniel Priestley
- Tony Robbins
- Adrian Savage
- Tony Selimi
- Zoe Socrates
- Mike Southon
- Anthony Stears
- Alan Stevens
- Barnaby Wynter

CONTENTS

Introduction 8

Chapter 1 The REAL Leader's Current Challenges 13

Chapter 2 Moving From "Compete" to "Complete" 23

Chapter 3 Winning by Thinking 44

Chapter 4 Improving the Quality of Your Thinking 57

Chapter 5 Positive Intention Leads to Positive Impact 73

Chapter 6 How to Be a Centerpreneur 85

Chapter 7 Making Milestones Matter 95

Chapter 8 The Thoughtful Leader Takes Risks Thoughtfully 103

Chapter 9 Being Truly Thoughtful
(thinking of others) –
Baring, Sharing and Daring
to Care 108

Chapter 10 You Can Learn to Care 121

Chapter 11 Thinking Bigger 129

Conclusion 134

Introduction

Leaders have to deal with a multitude of challenges: maintaining a vision that others can follow, setting the pace and tone for the business or business unit, and in many cases managing people, budgets and conflicting agendas and priorities. Inspiring others is usually found at the bottom of the list, in the "nice to have" category, as long as everything else is handled. However, deep down, most leaders would like to be more inspirational. Perhaps to be what is called a "thought leader", if that is not too lofty a goal.

Thought leadership has become part of the business vernacular, but it is such an overused term that it really has begun to lose its meaning. Most of what is published or presented as thought leadership is nothing of the kind. In my book *24 Carat BOLD*, I presented a model whereby aspiring thought leaders could create a strategy, measure their effectiveness and do specific things to share their best ideas and become recognized for them. Since then, I have shared that model in presentations, training and coaching, with thousands of business owners, executives and aspiring thought leaders. It still works as a framework for assessing and developing your own thought leadership.

When Seth Godin called *24 Carat BOLD* "the first thoughtful book I've seen on what it means to become a thought leader" it did not occur to me that the word "thoughtful" was, in fact, the key to the entire concept. Six years later, I have found myself coming back over and over again to the idea of "thoughtfulness", and recently realized this completely encapsulates my current thinking. It is what I care about most (and as you will learn in this book, caring counts for a lot!), it is what I do and what I am really interested in doing for the rest of my life: encouraging thoughtful leadership.

Being bold and exhibiting the attributes of REAL thought leadership are certainly important, and working with the REAL model can give you clarity and raise your profile. Practicing thoughtful leadership goes much further and allows really special people with really special ideas to be seen and appreciated.

Before we begin, let me be very clear about what I mean by thoughtful, since there are several meanings. Here are some dictionary definitions of the word thoughtful:

thoughtful (adjective) [thawt-*fuh* l]

1. showing consideration for others; considerate.

2. characterized by or manifesting careful thought: *a thoughtful essay*.

3. occupied with or given to thought; contemplative; meditative; reflective: *in a thoughtful mood*.

4. careful, heedful, or mindful: *to be thoughtful of one's safety*.

Thoughtful Leadership

What we can see is that there are two main meanings of the word thoughtful. One has to do with thinking and the other pertains to consideration for other people. In other words, one has to do with the head, and the other with the heart. I thought it was important to explore both of these concepts fully in this book because a thoughtful leader embodies and exhibits both of these skills.

Each chapter has a short title and an inspirational quotation to set the mood. Inspirational quotations are great because they capture important thoughts succinctly and often cleverly. They also tend to go viral. One of my dreams is that my best sound bites are shared widely, that they "go viral". But as you will learn in this book and my other material, going viral is not random, nor is it an accident. You have to put really exciting ideas out in a simple and shareable format.

Therefore, the first paragraph of each chapter (sometimes just the first sentence) is the core message or "thought" of that chapter. This is a discipline I teach my clients, and I absolutely wanted to practice what I preach. Besides, putting the book together in this way ensured that I had the clarity of thought before launching into the full explanation of each idea.

It also means that if you are short on time, or have an attention deficit disorder, you can grasp the essence of each chapter quickly. And if you like the thought for that chapter, you have something interesting to tweet! I have also placed my favorite sound bites in easy-to-spot boxes, called Thought Bites, so feel free to tweet them, ideally crediting me at @MindyGK.

Being somewhat involved in the book world, I know the trend is for shorter books, and I have aimed to keep this book as short as possible, while still covering all the key points. If you are seeking more in-depth information and discussion on any of these points, simply get in touch with me. I'm very easy to find online, and happy to speak to people offline – by phone or in person – as I travel around the world sharing these ideas. I look forward to hearing from you! This information is repeated at the end of the book, for ease of use.

Connect with me:

My websites:
www.thethoughtfulleader.com
www.mindygk.com
www.bookmidwife.com
www.panomapress.com

LinkedIn:
www.uk.linkedin.com/in/mindy.gibbinsklein

YouTube:
www.youtube.com/user/bookmidwife

Twitter:
www.twitter.com/bookmidwife and
www.twitter.com/MindyGK

Facebook: www.facebook.com/mindy.gibbinsklein

Phone numbers (what a novel idea!):
UK +44 (0) 8345 003 8848 or USA +1 (855) 883-1202

Chapter 1

The REAL Leader's Current Challenges

"Self-worth comes from one thing - thinking that you are worthy."

Wayne Dyer

Who on earth would sign up to be a leader? It is fraught with challenges and offers no guarantees. The balancing act of being responsible for other people's livelihoods and welfare, as well as achieving business targets, working more hours than ever, in an increasingly stressful environment and society… it's madness. However, the glory of building something important, something to be proud of: that's the thing that keeps most entrepreneurs, executives and leaders going. If you are a leader today, getting the balance to work in your favor is key, and keeping yourself strong and confident is the first step.

The leader's confidence must be protected

Just about every leader and entrepreneur I've met, underneath their successful façade, has a pretty fragile ego. Their sense of self-worth tends to be attached to their business, their idea or their success, especially if they started the business or built up the department or business unit. I began to suspect that under the surface, a lot of fear and doubt still existed, and I had some interesting conversations over the past few years.

Then I conducted a survey with a wider group, to see if my suspicions were correct. I found that although people still felt creative, a surprisingly large number of business owners, more than half, after two years in business, were less confident about success and less happy than when they started and more than half were occasionally or regularly thinking of quitting because it was not working out.

Do you feel more or less confident and happy than when you first started your business? Answer this question honestly, even if you never share the answer with anyone else. If things are not going the way you want with your business, you can begin to shift it in any direction you choose, starting right now. Drop anyone else's measure of success and assess your real feelings. If your own sense of self-worth has started to take a hit, it's just that you are so intimately linked with the business and you may have forgotten that your ego does not have to be in charge. In fact, if you overcompensate and lead with your ego, you may appear arrogant and actually push success away.

Much has been written about ego or arrogance, and many people criticize and condemn those who seem to exhibit an overabundance of it. It tends to show up as approval-seeking, where someone constantly looks for validation for their actions and their achievements. If you take the time to look into this phenomenon – either in your own behavior or that of others – you will soon discover the reasons behind it.

Insecurity comes from fear of not being enough and fear of not being loved. Tony Robbins talks about these two fears, which are apparently at the root of every other fear we have. This means that many people worry about not being good enough or loved enough. When you are in charge of a business or team, you can feel afraid of failure because it will reflect badly on you and your leadership skills. You may also be worried about the effects failure could have on others who depend on you for their livelihood. If you do not have any staff, it tends to be the former.

Excessive attention-seeking is very different from self-worth. People with high as well as low self-worth can both come across as needy and desperate for attention. Having been involved in professional training, speaking and coaching organizations for the past ten years, I have met many individuals who like to talk about themselves and what they do. Some, unfortunately, go too far with it, making them look desperate.

One of the authors I published several years ago was always promoting himself and his book online. Self-promotion, as you will read about later in the book, is important to let your market know what you do and what you offer. However, it can be overdone and upset people. In the case of this author, I tried to coach him on having a balance and creating other messages, so not every communication was promotional in nature. But he consistently overdid the self-promotion. No one else said anything to him about it, so he thought I was just being over-cautious. I could look at book sales and social media engagement, and I could read between the lines of other people's comments. This guy was hurting his success by appearing overanxious and desperate. The more he boosted his own profile, the more people pulled away. A mutual friend confided in me that they had to unfollow and disconnect from my client's profiles because it was all getting too much.

What if that were you? How would you feel if people were actively trying to avoid you and your endless boasting and bragging? Have you seen people constantly promoting themselves, their work and their business, without adding valuable content?

Maybe they are just trying to become the top dog and they don't know the best way to go about it.

Top Dog Syndrome

You may have heard of the expression "top dog" in either a positive or negative context. In fact, my good friend Andy Bounds has just come out with a new book called *Top Dogs* (co-authored with Richard Ruttle), which shows how to negotiate and deal with people in power, and avoid becoming an underdog in your communications! The book is specifically about power games in communications, but what I'm talking about is when people go too far, or become obsessed with achieving top dog status, at any cost.

So let's talk about dogs for a moment. Dogs mark out their territory by urinating on it. That's a nice image for you, isn't it? So, if you want be a top dog, you will need to lift your leg – metaphorically speaking. Personally, I think there are better ways to shine and succeed with your personal gifts and talents. Some people make a habit of elbowing people out of the way, trying to make others look bad, stepping all over them on their way to the top. I saw a lot of this when I worked in the corporate world, and it didn't give me a warm and fuzzy feeling.

> **Thought Bite:** If you want be a top dog, you will need to lift your leg @MindyGK

I don't think you need to lift your leg to get to where you want to be. But you do probably need to put one foot in front of the other and take a few steps, perhaps in a different direction. You will see what I mean as we go through the strategies in this book.

Sticking with the dog metaphor for a moment, I'd like you to consider the behavior of dogs in packs. Most of the dogs are happy to follow the lead dog, and they don't always get the chance or even want to be the lead dog. I spoke about this a lot in *24 Carat BOLD*. It's OK if you don't have a great desire to be a leader with lots of followers. This book is intended to inspire you to be a better leader of yourself and those in your immediate sphere of influence. If you choose to expand that, it's up to you. But don't let anyone tell you there is something wrong with being part of the pack.

One final example using dogs, then I promise we will spend most of our time talking about humans. What happens when a dog has been kicked too many times? When a dog has been kicked over and over, it usually begins to flinch and run away when it perceives a new threat. The learned response comes from having been treated badly. If you have tried to succeed and failed, or things have not worked out the way you thought or desired, it may be tempting to give up and not try again.

> **Thought Bite:** Don't let anyone tell you there is something wrong with being part of the pack @MindyGK

However, you may just want to picture a Golden Retriever as he steps out of a lake, gives himself a shake (spraying water everywhere) and looks for his next adventure. If you're going to be a dog, this is a good one to model.

Putting people on a pedestal

Many people believe that others really are better, or better off, smarter, happier or just plain luckier than they are. Those beliefs may or may not be true, and maintaining them and holding others up can actually keep you down. I'm not suggesting you shouldn't admire people who have achieved great things. They can inspire you and act as role models, proof of what is possible. Just be aware of any tendency to dwell too long on other people.

My mother has always said don't envy or wish you were someone else, you'd have to take their whole life, everything about it, good and bad. And we really have no idea what others are going through.

We compare ourselves to others, and even when we think we are better than the other person, there is always that feeling that we could be overtaken.

In my line of work, I see a lot of aspiring authors and speakers. The ones who spend a lot of time looking at and envying others miss the point. The point is that the other entrepreneur, speaker or author had their own challenges and route to get where they are today. They also have things going on in their lives that they don't share widely, or actively hide. Such as financial worries, personal relationship problems, health challenges… the list goes on.

Be careful about comparisons in general, since they are often fraught with assumptions and misconceptions. We will discuss this in more detail in the next chapter.

Putting yourself on a pedestal

Social media and the Internet in general have a lot to answer for, making it acceptable and even encouraging people to "big themselves up"! I cringe when I look at a business professional's LinkedIn profile and it says "Expert", or even "Guru" (yes, really!), or "Thought Leader". We all know the person crafted that profile themselves, so they are claiming to be those things. Self-proclaimed thought leadership is discounted by the people who are subjected to it, and many times it would not meet the definition of thought leadership at all.

Now, perhaps I am partly at fault for speaking and writing over the past six years about being a thought leader. Many people have read my book *24 Carat BOLD* and felt inspired to claim their position as a thought leader in their space. However, at no point did I ever give people permission, or even encourage them, to call themselves thought leaders! Think about it. It's like walking up to someone and saying, "I'm great. Look how great I am. Look how special I am." You just wouldn't do it. At least, I hope you wouldn't do that.

> **Thought Bite:** Self-proclaimed thought leadership is discounted by the people who are subjected to it @MindyGK

One of my authors, Julia Felton, is a sincere, hard-working leadership development coach and trainer. She runs equine inspired leadership programs, where people learn about themselves and improve team dynamics by working with horses. Her award-winning experience and her book *Unbridled Success* have raised Julia's profile and resulted in work with leaders in different countries. A reader in Japan was so impressed with the content of the book that she flew to the UK to work with Julia personally!

Despite being excellent at what she does, Julia remains humble and even a bit understated. Maybe it's all the time spent with her horses... Seriously, I wanted to showcase Julia here since she deserves it and doesn't do too much promotion herself.

Where would you put yourself on the self-promotion scale?

Not enough   **Just about right**   **Too much**
|————————————————|————————————————|

If you don't know how you appear to your clients or your market, perhaps it is time to do a survey where people can tell you what they think of you and the way you come across. I'd recommend you let them answer the questions anonymously.

Chapter 2

Moving From "Compete" to "Complete"

"Thousands of candles can be lighted from a single candle, and the life of the candle will not be shortened."

Buddha

Several years ago, I did a presentation called "Don't Seek Unique" which touched on many of these themes and asked people to stop worrying about what everyone else was doing. An executive came up to me after the talk and said he had never even considered *not* comparing himself to others, and that competitive research and market research were a major part of how his business operated. But he was excited about trying something new...

In *24 Carat BOLD* and many of the talks I give, I compare running a business and building a brand to running in a race. You have your own race to win, but you may be tempted to look around you, ahead of you and even behind you, to see what others are doing. It can be motivational, but it can also distract you from the business of running your race, and it can even trip you up.

A particularly relevant "race" occurs for many of my clients on a daily basis. It's called Amazon rankings. Over the past few years, it has become almost de rigueur to aspire to become an Amazon "'bestseller". Amazon encourages this by ranking all books on their sites. The emphasis on bestseller status has skewed the real picture and has led to all kinds of gamification, which even my clients have engaged in, just to get to that Number 1 slot. With Amazon regularly updating the rankings, checking can become an obsession, causing authors to lose sleep, agonize over the number, and even embarrass themselves with too much online promotion and communication. And all the while, the ranking is getting diluted and devalued, as more and more authors compete in this game.

As much as I understand this is a trend and even a marketing strategy now, and as I said, we do participate in it when the author really wants to (I will probably do a few campaigns for this book, in fact!), I still encourage my clients to focus on "best book" rather than "bestseller". I mean, if you put out any old content, you can get it to the top with marketing strategies, but once people start reading it and critiquing it, the real value of your content will be obvious to the world. It's not just about the numbers. If you focus on creating the best book – and by book I mean all your content – then you will improve your chances of becoming an organic bestseller and a highly respected thoughtful leader in the process.

Looking at your book ranking (or your Alexa ranking, Klout score or any other measure, in fact) all encourage a focus on comparison, and even a seasoned thought leader or author's feeling of self-worth can rise and fall like the tide.

Is it really true that there can only be one winner? No! There's lots of room for lots of winners, each adding value in their own way. We do not really compete. But sometimes when you see someone else in your industry doing well, it can feel like you have been stabbed in the gut, like someone has taken what is yours and given it to someone else. Taken food right out of your mouth, especially when you have bills to pay and you find out that the client you were counting on has decided to work with someone else.

Actually, it doesn't usually take anything away from you when someone else does well. Even in the most competitive industries, hundreds and thousands of similar businesses survive. So why this need to be the only one? In part it is societal conditioning, and in part it is psychological. Let's explore both of these areas in more depth.

Success is a double-edged sword

Here is a common leadership story. You set out to become successful. You work really hard, you build your reputation, you do good work and put out great content. You become a leader in your organization or industry. You then look for the next challenge. Perhaps you need something bigger, and you certainly need to protect your current achievement. The pressure builds. You need more and more success, more and more recognition. You have more to lose, farther to fall. You feel you can't afford to fail; everyone is watching.

Before you reach the heady levels of success, you want to be seen and heard. Everyone tells you that's the goal. Be seen and heard. Be visible and vocal. Be the thought leader. However, in the quest to achieve thought leadership requires you to stand out. Many authors, including me, have written about standing out, making your mark and being a true thought leader.

But there is a paradox between wanting to be special and unique, and at the same time wanting to fit in with a community and be accepted. We do like to feel special and unique, but very few people want to be so different from everyone else that they have no one to whom they can relate or with whom they can build trusted relationships. So we seek common ground. We don't want to lose those connections. So the thoughtful leader spends time balancing these two aspirations, and often teeters on the continuum.

Discontentment

The same goes for the continuum between contentment and discontentment. There is nothing wrong with being discontent with the way things are and striving to change and improve your situation, your results and even the world. Discontentment creates a starting point for change. It is the sand or grit that can start to form the pearl in the oyster.

What have I done for you lately?

There is one more interesting dichotomy for leaders today. It involves the internal battle between our selfish, self-centered tendencies and our desire to be more collaborative and abundant. One of the best ways to achieve both is to look for ways to collaborate that benefit you or your business. Referring non-competitive business to other colleagues puts you in a great position – the position of "giver" – and creates a desire in the other person's mind to pay you back in some way. Having been a director of BNI, the world's largest referral organization, I am a big believer in actively looking out for and giving referrals to other people. I am not going to elaborate on referral techniques here; for in-depth information, look up books and other resources from my good friends and clients Charlie Lawson (author of *The Unnatural Networker*) and Andy Lopata (author of several books including *And Death Came Third* and *Recommended!*)

What I do want to stress here is that you need to be seen as a helpful referrer or introducer. Really look for the best person or company to serve your client, if you can't be the one to get the business. Only refer one person or business to meet the need. There's nothing worse than receiving a referral where you are immediately competing with another person or business, simply because the introducer named both of you, as if you were equal (which you are not). When referring business, the thoughtful leader takes the extra time and care to refer only *one* company, the best one for the client.

As I mentioned in the Introduction, the word thoughtful has two meanings: one has to do with putting thought into something, and the other has more to do with caring. What I didn't mention earlier is that I am a fluent speaker of Spanish. It is my second language, and I sometimes call myself bilingual. Why am I bringing this up now? Because in Spanish there are two separate words for the word thoughtful. Many other languages make the distinction also. It's only English that tries to use the same word for these very different concepts. However, in this case, it works in our favor, since leaders today can achieve a blend of both for an even more successful outcome.

With the amount of noise in the form of millions of blogs, videos, articles, posts and even books, what is needed now more than ever is good quality thoughts and ideas – real thoughts. Ironically real thoughts are often the missing component in what is called "thought leadership". No real thought goes into it.

Does the thoughtful leader always get it right? No. But they have the right intention and are willing to try again and improve the quality.

You can teach people to think. You may think this happens at school, but I am talking about real analytical thinking, philosophical thinking, critical thinking.

Up until recently, I thought the Internet and the ease with which you can find information and answers was a good thing. I mean, it is good, but it can also be a curse, a time and energy drain, a rat hole and a depressing, endless obsession. If you are trying to build your business, you do need to be actively marketing it, and that includes social media activity. However, some people have addictive personalities and they can get distracted and lose a lot of time reading irrelevant information or getting caught up in others' news and dramas. If it doesn't lead to any new insights or ideas that can enhance your own thinking and content, then it has very little value.

The more you focus on others, the more you may doubt yourself and slow your own progress. I love this comment from prominent thought leader James Altucher, as it sums up the issue perfectly:

> Your competition is not other people but the time you kill, the ill will you create, the knowledge you neglect to learn, the connections you fail to build, the health you sacrifice along the path, your inability to generate ideas, the people around you who don't support and love your efforts, and whatever god you curse for your bad luck.

Be careful about being influenced by others' thoughts and ideas

You will always be exposed to outside influences but you don't have to be a pinball in a machine, being moved by external forces outside your control. You are not one of Pavlov's dogs.

To be an expert in something, you have to know a lot about it. It is important to read others' ideas on your topic, watch videos and listen to other speakers on the subject, but you also have to do it, experience it, practice it, and refine it. Whether you need

10,000 hours of experience and practice to become an expert, or whether it is a different measure, there is certainly a way to assess people's expertise and thought leadership by depth of thinking, and original thinking.

There are dangers in reading and absorbing too much on your topic.

1. You begin to regurgitate others' thoughts and ideas so you don't sound original.

2. You risk accidentally plagiarizing others and their work, which is usually unintentional but still very dangerous. I have seen books taken out of print due to issues like this.

3. You become so impressed with the ideas you are reading that a nagging thought begins to enter your mind. It sounds something like this: "Wow, that is so good. They know so much. They've said it all. It's all been said and done. I don't have anything new to add to this..." This is like number 1 but it is internally focused.

The other insidious influence on your thinking and your self-esteem is social media. I love social media for what it has brought to entrepreneurs and people in general. It has never been easier to spread ideas fast, connect with long-lost friends or simply feel you are not alone.

But when some people spend excessive amounts of time online, they risk a few things. The first is FOMO which stands for Fear of Missing Out. This is a new 21st century problem, which occurs when you see people you know posting about the amazing nights out they've had or holidays they've been on. Or other posts about deals being won, new clients and successful business ventures.

Whether or not those posts are absolutely accurate, or possibly misleading or exaggerated, the effect is the same. It causes people to feel inadequate, like they are missing out on something, and their own lives and achievements are not good enough. Do you see how it often comes down to that worry or concern about not being good enough?

The dubious value of competition

I have two friends who always forward me emails and articles written by people who are doing similar things to me. They think they are being helpful. They usually include a note that says "so you know what they're up to." Thanks, but no thanks. I don't really want to know what those so-called competitors are up to. Not only does it take precious time away from my own creative activities, but it churns me up inside, makes me doubt my beautiful business, brand, product and secure proposition and even myself. That might sound crazy to people who know me to be very self-confident. Well, one of the ways in which I remain confident is to actively avoid or even ignore information about others in my industry.

Competition seems to be increasing exponentially these days. Or maybe it is simply the RAS (reticular activating system) kicking in. The RAS is a part of your brain that helps you notice more of what you are focused on. This means that when you think of something, like a particular brand, you begin to see more and more of it everywhere you go.

Whether it is real or imagined, when you are reacting to things and not being a thoughtful leader, it can seem like you are constantly trying to deal with new threats and competitors' actions. In a meeting of professional speakers last year, we agreed that handling the seemingly exponential growth in copycat content and even outright stealing was becoming a bit like the Whack-a-Mole game. You know the one where you have to hit the mole on the head (sorry to my pacifist and vegetarian friends) and every time you hit the mole, another one pops up? It can feel a bit like that if you are in a competitive sort of industry.

A business owner I know fairly well shared something really interesting with me recently. She said she hated seeing all the great things everyone else was doing, that they seemed to be doing better and achieving more success than her. I was touched by her honesty and vulnerability, but I was saddened that she was allowing these feelings to hijack her emotions and sabotage all of her excellent efforts in business.

The feeling of inadequacy made her want to give up, just when success was within reach. It didn't matter how good her last month or quarter had been; she was comparing herself to other people and feeling like she didn't measure up. What astounded me, and I have seen other people do this, is that she wasn't even working with any facts or figures, but rather a *perception* that the others were doing well, or doing better than she was. This lady became tearful when she shared this story with me so I knew it really hurt. I told her what I'm about to tell you: Don't look! Don't watch!

My nephew, when he was about a year old, was at the zoo with his grandparents (my parents) when they stopped next to the elephant enclosure. The big beasts scared him so he put his blanket over his eyes. My mother thought that was clever of him. I thought maybe it would have been easier if he had just closed his eyes instead, but he was only one and didn't think of that! Anyway, he instinctively knew something that perhaps we all need to re-learn: if you don't like watching something and it doesn't make you feel good, don't watch!

Why would you do things that make you feel bad?

You may know someone who picks at a scab until it bleeds. It hurts! Why would they do that? Is it masochism? Do they actually like to feel pain? I don't think so.

When I was a teenager, I used to get a lot of sore throats. Sometimes my throat was so painful it felt like I was swallowing burning lava. I remember swallowing every few minutes to see if my throat was still sore. I knew it was going to be sore, and I knew it was going to hurt, but something inside me made me do it over and over.

> **Thought Bite:** If you don't like watching something and it doesn't make you feel good, don't watch! @MindyGK

If you have ever had a sore tooth, you may know what I'm talking about. Did you find yourself poking that tooth regularly to see if it still hurt? Of course it is still going to hurt, if it hurt when you poked it ten minutes earlier.

You know it is going to hurt, but you keep checking, just in case.

Partly, it is habit or even addiction. I believe

many of us do quite a few things on a regular basis that don't make us feel very good. For example, I know coffee really affects me and causes me to wake up early, and salt causes me to feel bloated, but I often consume both of these things.

There is also a fear that you will miss something if you do not check Facebook or other platforms on a regular basis. As I mentioned earlier, FOMO has entered our vocabulary as a real fear. There has been much written on this phenomenon, which has always been there, but occurs so much faster and more regularly with the speed of social media and the quantity of content being shared.

We have become, as well as an egoistic culture, a voyeuristic one. Half of our time is spent promoting ourselves, showing off, worrying about how others will view us, while the other half of the time we are listening, watching and making judgments about others, in more detail than ever before. This happens because people are sharing more and more intimate details about themselves than ever before.

The noisiness of the online world is matched only by the nosiness of people online!

Stop!

Stop looking, stop torturing yourself. Stop poking that tooth. Focus on something else if you can. Hopefully, by the end of this book, you will have plenty of other things to focus on – things that can get you closer to your leadership and life goals.

> **Thought Bite:** The noisiness of the online world is matched only by the nosiness of people online! @MindyGK

Unplug and see what happens. I am pretty sure the world won't end if you are offline for a few hours or even a few days. There is a book I've heard about but not read, called *The Winter of Our Disconnect*. What a clever title, wish I'd thought of it! Anyway, I believe it is the story of a single mother with teenage kids who unplugged the whole family from devices, television, Internet and other electronic stimuli for a period of several months. This may be making you come out in a cold sweat just thinking about it, but apparently, after a period of adjustment, this family discovered the simple joys of life, and spending time with each other, and there was a happy ending.

Maybe it is not possible, with the demands of your business, work or other commitments, to disconnect for a long period of time, but there could be great benefits in store for you with just a short rest from it all. I see several friends each week consciously going offline, and telling the world they won't be available for a day or two, or a week. They always surface on the other side more peaceful and ready to face the world again.

Woowoo Warning

I'd like to protect you from all of the craziness, if you will let me. It involves taking a few minutes (unplugged) and doing a short exercise. Imagine wrapping yourself up in a soft blanket. Feel yourself curl up and feel protected and warm. Breathe evenly and slowly for a couple of seconds. Bring a smile to your face and feel secure in your blanket.

Or imagine a bubble around you, something to keep you quite safe and secure. This bubble can muffle the sounds, sights and textures of the outside world, as much or as little as you like. Have you ever tried to listen to sounds under water? Imagine your bubble softening and absorbing all the noise, so you just get a peaceful sense of floating. Your bubble allows in only those things that serve and support you. You can control when and how your bubble expands to cover you, and how much it filters out.

You may want to do the exercises I just described, even for 30 seconds. I think you would do well to repeat the exercises and the feelings you create on a regular basis. But of course that is up to you.

Whether or not you do "woowoo" exercises like the one I've just outlined, you do need to keep your own confidence and self-esteem as high as possible if you want to achieve your highest potential and help others. There is absolutely no point wasting time feeling less than adequate because you have allowed others to take the podium, or even put them there yourself.

Competence, competition and "competension"!

When you first decide you are competent at something and you throw your hat in the ring as an expert or specialist or whatever you call yourself, you are setting off down a path. That path could get more crowded as you progress, the opposite of a marathon where all the runners are jammed together at the beginning and then the crowd thins out as the race progresses.

First you notice the competition (or not, depending on how you respond to this book), and if left unchecked, the pressure of maintaining your position of expert and remaining ahead of the competition can build. I found that in the early days before my micro-niche of book coaching got more crowded, I never really thought about other people who did similar things. In fact, it gave me a great sense of pride to be doing something that I had never seen anyone else doing before. In the early years, there weren't many people in "my" industry, and I was happily serving all the clients that came my way, without comparing myself to anyone else. Life was good.

Competence → Competition → Competension

Then, as the business grew more successful, I began to notice others entering the space, and this created some interesting feelings in me. At times, I felt upset, threatened, angry, jealous and even depressed. At least five of these "copycats" had worked with me, attended my programs, learned my content and they were now setting up their own businesses in exactly the same space.

On days when I felt strong, I was able to put things in perspective. My own business was improving all the time and nobody else was doing things in the exact way I did them. No one could ever be me.

So why was I even thinking about my competitors, much less worrying about them? It seems illogical, and it can remain unconscious until it creeps up on you and shocks you. But then, as your awareness grows, you can find yourself spending time dwelling on these other folks. As I said earlier, you may imagine them stealing your clients and your business; you may picture them as evil imposters, taking food out of your children's mouths… OK, maybe we are going too far. Or are we? When I speak to some of my colleagues about their competition, they do get embroiled in this sort of thinking and it causes a lot of angst and fear for them, which is very real.

I have created a word for the negative pressure of trying to stay at the top, and stay on top of your competitors: COMPETENSION.

> **Thought Bite:** Competension:
> The negative pressure of trying to stay at the top, and stay on top of your competitors @MindyGK

This made-up word sums up for me all the emotional connotations of pitting yourself against others in a win-lose situation.

We don't like losing. Well, I have never met anyone who likes losing! They may exist though...

I actually know exactly why I hate losing. I don't like losing because it reminds me of running in a race when I was nine years old, and I was one of the last to finish. I'm not sure why I was not a good runner or a fast runner in those days, as I had pretty long legs. But I had not trained for this particular race and I had no aerobic endurance at all.

Over the next few weeks and months, the other children saw that I was a slow runner and not very athletic, and so I became one of the last ones to be picked for teams. This kind of negative reference can stay with you for a long time, and even though it makes no sense at all to take a school sports reference into adult professional life, this is the kind of thing that your subconscious can do to you.

In NLP (Neuro-Linguistic Programing) terms, we have certain anchors that were created at some point in the past, and there are triggers which can set off a reaction, sometimes subconsciously and sometimes more consciously. Every human being has triggers that set off reactions. The more extreme the emotion around the issue, the more extreme the reaction may be.

In my case, I run for my own sense of achievement and fitness nowadays, and when I do run in a race or half marathon, I am not competing or comparing myself to others. I aim for the best time I can do, for my level of fitness and training. It's much more gratifying, for me. Others may really enjoy competition, but not me.

Woowoo Warning

If you dare, find and work with a trained NLP practitioner and get to the bottom of any negative anchors that are holding you back and triggers that set you off. Even if you are not completely aware of them, or able to articulate exactly what they are or why they are causing you issues, you can still collapse these anchors and achieve much more and much faster. If you need a referral to a qualified NLP professional, coach or therapist, just ask me. I know a lot of good ones.

Chapter 3

Winning by Thinking

*"Thinking is like loving and dying.
Each of us must do it for himself."*

Josiah Royce

One way to cope with a tough marketplace or increased competition is to get determined to win, and I can always find examples of people putting themselves into competitive situations and tackling the "enemy" head-on. This is more of a masculine approach, going into battle. The more feminine approach is to shrink back.

The approach I and many of my colleagues seem to have taken is neither of these. Better to constantly redefine the space so that there is no real competition. You are a category of one. The moment it looks like someone else is doing or saying something similar to me, I immediately look for points of differentiation.

As I mentioned in the last chapter, for many years there was very little competition in the book coaching space here in the UK. I went about my business, doing my best work, enjoying myself and feeling like I was creating something truly unique. Then, little by little, over the years, a number of other people began to show up offering similar services.

> **Thought Bite:** Constantly redefine the space so that there is no real competition @MindyGK

Some of these were people whom I had trained or coached personally and it made me very angry to see them encroaching on "my" market with "my" content and ideas. I approached one or two of them directly, but of course I could not order them to stop providing their service. In my mind, they were copying me, ripping off my ideas. In their minds, they were just starting a new business (for them) and they thought it was different or even better than what I had to offer.

So here's what I learned. There is no such thing as Intellectual Property. Let me explain. You don't really own anything in the area of thought leadership. Every idea can and probably will be copied. In fact, ideas that you think are yours can probably be found in other people's work dating back many hundreds or even thousands of years. You can expend a lot of energy and worry thinking about protecting ideas which are not able to be protected.

IP = It's Public

The only ways I know of to actually protect yourself and your ideas are by obtaining trademarks, copyrights and patents. Most ideas that we have are not going to be deemed "trademark-able". You have to have something really, really original and different to qualify. Plus, you would have to pay. A lot.

How do I know this? We actually went through the process of trademarking The Book Midwife® in several geographic regions. We trademarked the name as it pertains to book coaching. The main reason we had the trademark approved is that the term "book midwife" is not a real phrase that someone would say in a normal conversation. The trademark folks called it "whimsical", which means it is not a real concept. So you can't say "she is *a* book midwife". It's a brand and I find it worthy of protecting.

Protection costs money, and in my businesses we budget for things like legal fees. Over the years, we have only had to contact a few people who didn't understand that the term was trademarked. They all apologized, and in two cases we found a way to collaborate with the other people for mutual benefit.

I have many, many ideas around the area of books, writing, publishing and promotions that I would not even try to protect because they are just that: ideas. Instead of spending even more time and money trying to protect everything under the sun, I choose to spend my time and energy creating more and more lovely services and products – like this book!

Practical things you can do

You can stop people copying your material verbatim with plagiarism detection tools. Plagiarism means copying content word for word. It is not the same as paraphrasing or talking about similar ideas. As I mentioned above, ideas are very, very difficult to protect. But if you have gone to the effort of creating good quality written content (articles, blogs, ebooks and books in print), other people should not be allowed to steal it or pass it off as their own.

You can keep creating more great content. Yes, this requires a certain amount of effort and consistent work. But the best thinkers don't just have one thought and then sit around for the rest of their lives. They are constantly coming up with new ideas and getting them out into the world by writing, publishing and speaking (the only way to share ideas widely). The very best thinkers wrap all of their content into one strong theme or concept, which they can become known for.

Greg and Fiona Scott travel the world, running their business virtually and effectively. The authors of the highly acclaimed, award-winning book *Living a Laptop Lifestyle* practice what they preach and really do live that laptop lifestyle. They didn't stop at a full-length book, but constantly produce new material on their theme, in the form of articles, blogs, videos and social media posts. They epitomize this idea of creating lots of content to build a substantive profile for your thought leadership. If you aspire to be a thoughtful leader, you will build time into your busy schedule to come up with good, thoughtful content on a regular basis.

You can learn and practice the ideas in the next chapter to come up with better and more exciting ideas and concepts. A key issue we will address in the next chapter is quality of thought. It is my belief that many people are lazy in their thinking or do not possess the skills needed for rigorous, in-depth thought and analysis. But I'm getting ahead of myself. We will explore this in depth in the very next chapter.

> **Thought Bite:** The best thinkers don't just have one thought and then sit around for the rest of their lives. @MindyGK

Attachment vs non-attachment

I think what executives, entrepreneurs and creative types really need to do is learn the way of non-attachment. This is a Buddhist concept, which states that all suffering occurs because of desire, and desire to hold on to things, people, memories and ideas that are actually impermanent.

When we experience lack or scarcity, we feel the gap between what we think we need or want and what we actually have. The irony is that the more we achieve and acquire, the more we stand to "lose". Fear of losing what you've got can be very strong, and probably directly proportional to the amount of effort or time it took you to achieve that goal or acquire that possession.

I know when I finally got my Lexus, after many years of planning, I was so scared to drive it for fear that something would happen to it. I still sometimes avoid driving it if I don't know where I am going to be able to park it. I don't want anything happening to my "baby". Completely irrational? Maybe, but this is my reality and I know how hard I worked to get that car.

In 24 Carat BOLD, I talk about very senior leaders having an extreme fear of failure because they have so much farther to fall. I imagine it is a similar fear that causes some celebrities to suffer from anxiety and depression. They believe that others have a greater expectation of them, as they are in the limelight. Everywhere they go, people are looking at what they are doing, how they are doing it, what they are saying. They don't want to let people down, but they especially don't want to let themselves down and lose everything they have fought so hard to achieve.

Even before you reach your goal, you can suffer from anxiety because of the perceived gap between what you have and what you want. Perhaps the thought of striving for such a massive outcome scares you. Or you may not believe that you can do it, or that you deserve it. Despite their fears, thoughtful leaders keep their focus on progress, not lack, and constantly move toward their goals.

At my first meditation retreat, I introduced myself to a fellow participant as a goals coach and goal-setting trainer. Well, that is what I was at the time. This person proceeded to call me "the goal setter" with quite negative connotations. Clearly, he believed that going for your goals was not congruent with the Buddhist principles.

> **Thought Bite:** Thoughtful leaders keep their focus on progress, not lack, and constantly move toward their goals @ MindyGK

Learn non-attachment. Learn to practice real gratitude for what you have instead of focusing on what you don't have. There have been many books and blogs written about gratitude, and I have heard people speak very eloquently on the subject. Therefore, I will keep this section short and point you to some other folks I think are worth listening to.

Non-attachment in business

I began to look for ways to differentiate myself, which I had never had to think about before. But even in thinking about how you differ from someone else in your industry, the first thing you need to do is look at what they are doing and what they are offering, so you can find those points of difference. And looking at what they are doing can bring up all the emotions I was talking about before!

> **Thought Bite:** Never stand still long enough for someone to copy you @ MindyGK

So stop focusing on being the best in your industry because that means you will need to be up to speed on the industry and where you rank within it. Then you will need to continually monitor where you rank and how and what everyone else is doing. You will need to spend precious time reading blogs, articles and books written by and about your competitors. I guarantee that at the end of that exercise you will feel worse, not better, about yourself, your business and your brand. You may be tempted to have thoughts such as "Look what they're doing!" "Oh, it's been done, it's been said already." "Oh, that looks/sounds/smells so much better than what we're doing/ saying/ producing." And on and on. And then, before you know it, you have that feeling that my entrepreneurial friend had – the one that makes you say "I feel like giving up. What's the point?"

Instead, keep your head down and produce more and more valuable content. Move on, move forward, move up the value chain. Never stand still long enough for someone to copy you.

Choose your influence and your influencers

So what should you be reading and watching? I can't give you the answer to that because everyone is different. I have some rules for myself, though, and I'll share them with you here, in case they are helpful.

What I do is ensure I spend on average an hour a day reading fiction, something that originated in the author's imagination. I like most fiction and appreciate historical fiction and even chick lit because the author has taken real situations and embellished or put their own spin and creativity into the mix. However, the best stimulant for my own imagination has always been science fiction and science fantasy. When I have been at my most creative, in life and in business, I have always had a science fiction or fantasy book on the go, prodding at my subconscious and causing me to expand my own thinking. These are genres where the author has asked the big questions, the very biggest questions. The ones that typically start with "What if…"

I will never forget when I worked with Simi Prasad, the author of the excellent YA novel *Out There*. Simi was 15 at the time, so you could say that she was still close enough to childhood to have a very active imagination. She really wanted to write dystopian fiction and though I don't normally work with this kind of book, her enthusiasm convinced me it would succeed.

We did a number of "What if" exercises, to get the creativity flowing. At one point, I prompted her with "What if men…" and she quickly finished the sentence "…didn't exist?" This became the core concept of the 90,000 word story, which Simi created in just a few months.

Non-fiction is also important, to keep you thinking about important concepts. You don't have to read full-length books all the time. Opinionated blogs and articles can also stimulate your thinking.

Inspirational books, blogs and articles

Most people do not read enough non-fiction, such as business books and especially self-help or personal development books. If you are reading this book, there is hope for you! Find out what else you can and should be reading, to improve your life and your business. Fill yourself up with positive, inspirational messages and content. Don't worry if the book or article you read sounds similar to something else you may have read. It probably does have some similar elements or ideas in it. After all, as I said earlier, there is little that is truly unique. That's not the point. Sometimes we need to read things several times, or even many times, to get the idea. We may need to hear things over and over again, perhaps in slightly different ways, to have them sink in. It's all about reinforcing positive ideas.

Feeding yourself

Do you have a good feed every day? That is, do you take advantage of the power of the Internet and get the best and most relevant content sent to your Inbox every day? I do. I use a tool called Feedspot, but there are plenty of others. It's a form of content curation, where the stories and blogs that you choose to see are served up to you each day, so you don't have to trawl though hundreds of sites to find them. My own "feed" brings me content written by Seth Godin, Penelope Trunk, Guy Kawasaki, James Altucher and several others. Having these "essential" blogs in one place ensures I see the best of the best, and it saves me a lot of time.

> **Thought Bite:** Sometimes we need to read things several times, or even many times, to get the idea @MindyGK

I also have inspirational videos and other news sent straight to me. The videos I value the most these days come from Upworthy and TED. You may have heard of Upworthy. It is an incredible platform for important ideas in the form of articles and videos. In a society that seems to extol sensationalism and bad news stories, it is refreshing to find a wealth of positive, uplifting and inspiring material all in one place.

You have probably heard of TED. It is a non-profit organization that was set up in 1984 to spread great ideas. The folks at TED believe, as I do, in spreading the most interesting and inspiring ideas from leading thinkers, as well as lesser-known experts. On the TED.com website, they say, "We believe passionately in the power of ideas to change attitudes, lives and, ultimately, the world." There is also TEDx now, a rapidly expanding network of local TED-style events, full of short presentations by experts in their fields. All leaders should be plugged into sites and events like these, to keep their thinking at the highest possible level, and their minds in a continuous state of curiosity. If you want to showcase your own ideas, TEDx or even TED should be a goal of yours. I was asked the other day if I had presented a TED talk and my answer was, "Not yet but soon."

Sign up for the daily notification from www.TED.com. Each video is only 17 or 18 minutes in length and highlights a unique perspective on a topic you may never have considered before. I find the content to be stimulating, thought-provoking and very inspiring. Well worth watching.

Chapter 4

Improving the Quality of Your Thinking

"No problem can withstand the assault of sustained thinking."

Voltaire

Really thinking things through

OK, so now you have read the books and articles. You have watched the videos. You have consumed lots of information on the subject you need to have ideas about. Time to do your own thinking now. That's right – your own thinking. Although you may be surprised to hear that you don't have to do your own thinking on your own. You can get help, you can discuss things with other people (sometimes called "thinking out loud") or you can clarify your thinking in journals, social media interactions and blog posts. The key thing is that you move from watching, reading and consuming, to crafting, producing and sharing.

Not content with content marketing

You may have heard of the term "content marketing". It has become very popular, and some people even equate it with thought leadership. Here is an excerpt from a popular LinkedIn article I wrote on this topic:

> I am not really content with the phrase "content marketing" to describe putting your best thoughts and ideas out into the world. First of all, content can mean anything and can be of dubious quality. All kinds of things can be called content. Even the phone book contains content.
>
> Secondly, marketing is too broad a discipline to describe sharing your key messages via writing, speaking and multimedia. Marketing strategies all depend on putting out some kind of content, so I don't see what the big deal is.
>
> And finally, business leaders don't really have time to do marketing of any kind, right? Some people believe that leaders should outsource time-consuming things like writing. But then what about speaking and videos? It's not yet possible to outsource those, just like it isn't possible to outsource your idea generation or

your thinking. Not if you really want to be an inspirational leader.

Very few people have time to sift through more and more material that adds little to no value or original thinking. The metaphor I used in *24 Carat BOLD* is finding a needle in an ever-increasing haystack, something sharp and to the point, yet very rare. The situation only seems to have worsened over the past five years.

So, what is the answer for the aspiring thought leader? A total, unapologetic commitment to discovering and delivering your very best, bold and opinionated messages. Messages that show people what you're really about. Messages that rock the boat if necessary. Every week, just a few articles, blogs and books really cut through the noise and impress me. I love finding those needles. I constantly challenge myself to put only needles into the market and not add to the haystack. Do I succeed every time? Of course not, but my intention is to get sharper all the time.

Please think about the way you use the word content. Content is everywhere; there's a glut of it and very little of it changes the world. Think twice and then think again before putting *any more* content out there. Shape and craft something truly interesting, amazing even. Something that others will call "thought leadership".

What if?

As you saw in the last chapter, some of the best questions start with "What if". It is a question we should ask more – of ourselves, of our situations, maybe even of the universe? It is a question that begins to stretch the boundaries of what's possible. It disrupts the standard or obvious response, which requires no thinking. Asking "what if" and several other important variants liberates your mind in ways that most people never experience.

So, even if you have a decent amount of clarity around your idea, test it by asking several different "what if" questions. For example:

> "What if it could only work in a certain way?"
>
> "What if it were inside out, upside down, backwards?"
>
> "What if the opposite were actually true?"
>
> "What if my life depended on this?"

Now, come up with at least three more prompts for your thinking, all starting with "What if…"

"What if…"

"What if…"

"What if…"

Push your thinking

"Push your thinking" is a term we use at my companies with our clients. It stands for pushing yourself, and it also implies that you don't allow yourself just one or two obvious responses to a question or solutions to an issue. If you found you could only come up with one or two answers to the above "What if" questions (if you even did the exercise!) then you may need to learn to push yourself a bit more. It only take a few minutes longer, and the more you push yourself, the more interesting and exciting answers you can come up with.

Don't settle for the easy answer or the cliché. If you have a mentor, a good coach or a mastermind group, you can get someone else to help you push your thinking and hold yourself accountable. Don't settle for anything less and don't let yourself off the hook! This is where you get traction and where you separate yourself from the pack as a thoughtful leader, sharing true thought leadership with the world.

There is a lot of lazy thinking or lack of thinking today. I got a card through my door the other day from a firm that sells houses. In the UK it's an estate agent; in the U.S. it's a real estate agent. The card invited me to contact them if I was thinking of selling my house. So far, so good. But the incentive they were offering was a chance to win six months' free gym membership. Hang on – I sell my house and move to a different area, so how can I use the gym membership? Maybe the offer is in conjunction with a nationwide gym network. As I'm not selling, I didn't check it out to find out how it works, but it just bothered me that it didn't make sense on the surface. It would have been better to offer something relevant and useful to someone moving house, such as a free moving van rental or cleaning service to get the old house in good shape before handing it over.

Helping others push their thinking

Once you become adept at pushing your thinking, it is your privilege and responsibility as a leader to show others how to do it. If you have had any challenges in your team, with lack of motivation, creativity, or enthusiasm, it could just be that your people are not exercising their thinking muscle. Leading by example, you will be in a position to show people within and outside your organization just how much fun you can have by spending that extra time on ideas and issues.

You should also consider setting up some guidelines and objectives for thinking things through to a greater degree. A few of my clients' organizations have implemented more rigor and structured thinking into their company cultures and it is really starting to pay off. To get the maximum benefit from this, you should document it in personal development plans, assessments, and internal communications. You can even reward people who have pushed their thinking and come up with better ideas and solutions. This will emphasize and further embed the importance of it into the company culture.

PLEASE think

Please think before you speak and certainly before you write something. I'm sorry if I am banging you over the head with this concept, but as I have said, sometimes we need to hear things a few times!

PLEASE is also an acronym I use when I am planning content, to make sure I am not just putting any old thing out there and adding to the noise. I thought everyone did this or something similar, but I have discovered that hardly anyone employs any real rigor in planning content. So, I'll share my model with you, in case it helps.

> P = Personal (Have I made it as personal as I can for the context?)

L = Less is More (Have I got the entire message across, without any excess?)

E = Engaging (Have I thought about how my reader likes to engage with me and my content?)

A = Answer (Have I answered a big question or concern for the reader? If not, it's just noise.)

S = Sync (Is this in sync with the rest of my content, my style, my profile?)

E = Exciting (Have I shared the most compelling information and used the most compelling wording possible?)

You have lots of thoughts; you need a good net to catch them

Is your problem that you have too many thoughts? Entrepreneurs and leaders do tend to get new ideas all the time, sometimes every day. This is only a problem if you feel the pressure to use them all or share them all, especially without any kind of control or process. You can also learn to think and assess fast without compromising the quality of your thinking. I was recently at a conference where I had a chat with someone and used a phrase that just popped into my head. They seemed to like it and really got what I was talking about. I knew I was on to something and I almost heard choirs of angels in my head!

As soon as I had the chance, I looked online to see if the domain was available. It was but it had a four-figure premium on the price (that's how good others thought the phrase was). But I needed to make a quick decision. I thought for just a few minutes, then grabbed the domain. I am now in the process of setting up an entirely new strand to my business, based on that phrase and that quick decision. Perhaps I could have just written it down and pondered the idea when I got back home from the conference. But maybe it would not have been available.

Control versus flow

Let's talk about control. It is a heavy word and has as much positive energy as negative energy. The "bad" aspects to it bring to mind excessive force, manipulation and even violence. However, controlling the impulse to insult someone, shout at someone or do something stupid, that can be a good thing. Control and willpower have helped many people get to a healthier weight and level of fitness, stop biting their nails, manage their anger and lots of other positive habits.

> **Thought Bite:** You need a strategy to quiet your mind from the chatter and noise that prevents you from hearing your own wisdom @MindyGK

It involves inserting a thought in between stimulus and response. I have read about it in many personal development and neuroscience books, and the first book that explained it really well for me was *The Seven Habits of Highly Effective People*, by the late Stephen Covey.

You need to get to the heart of what you really think and believe. Many people believe they don't know what they think. You can and should find out what you "stand for". It gives meaning to your life and work. If you need help with this, talk to me about our Inspiration Session that has helped over 1,000 people discover their core purpose, core message and strategy.

Get away!

If you can, put yourself into an environment that is optimized for creative thinking. This can be a week or two in a secluded and peaceful setting, a retreat where you get out of your normal routine and environment and come up with creative ideas, or develop some that never seem to progress. You can get help with this, for example retreats led by creative or strategic thinking facilitators. We run these at REAL Thought Leaders, so get in touch if you want to explore this.

It is not always possible or practical to go away on a retreat, course or vacation. Thinking by yourself, without help or guidance, takes quiet time and ideally a quiet space. Do you practice meditation on a regular basis? If not, you need some kind of strategy to quiet the mind from all the chatter and noise that prevents you from hearing your own wisdom.

When to do your best thinking

For most people, morning is the most productive and creative time, a time when they are fresh and the best ideas are flowing naturally. You can work with and enhance this natural rhythm by setting aside time in the morning to leverage this flow of ideas. I get fantastic ideas first thing in the morning, usually when I am up too early. For some reason, my body wakes up even though I feel I "should" be sleeping. I used to resent it, and try to get back to sleep.

Several months ago, I realized that I am not tired during the day, so I am probably getting enough sleep. Hint: listen to your body! I began to embrace this extra time, quiet time with no phones ringing or emails popping up. If it is an "acceptable" hour (5am is my own personal limit), I either lie very quietly in bed, so as not to disturb Phil, or I get up quietly.

I can capture my thoughts in my head and then, if appropriate, on paper.

Many people think you need to write everything down or you will lose it. Even I used to think that. But I have trained my mind to play with ideas and repeat the ones that resonate most loudly. Then I can write those down a few minutes or even a few hours later. The good ones and the ones you replay a few times stay in your mind and develop further. Of course, there is nothing wrong with having a notepad or tablet or phone by your bedside or wherever, to grab those ideas as they come to you. If you are really concerned that you won't remember the idea or the detail in the morning, you should take a moment to capture it when it occurs to you. However, I would advise against using voice recording or dictation at 5am when your partner is sleeping!

How long is a piece of thinking?

Firstly, I can't answer that question for you! Your thought process is different from others', so there is no one right way to do your thinking. However, I do have a number of tips, if you are at the point where you want to accelerate your thinking and increase your output. That is, get more done and more produced.

Having met thousands of people who thought about writing a book for many years, that thinking sometimes results in action and sometimes not. Or, more often than not, they do something about it. Many leaders tend to start a book or other important project, but not finish it. And until it is finished, it can't be published and create the profile-enhancing benefits that leader set out to achieve in the first place. Over the years, I have coached, mentored, cajoled, bullied, whipped and even bribed authors to finish their books, but there is only one person who can draw that line in the sand and say, "It's done. I'm ready to put it out there."

So the thinking phase is really important but you must not let it go on for too long. Over the years, I have had many clients go through a book writing process which is 90 days in length. Many, many people finish their final draft by the end of the program, so they are able to get it into editing and production. However, every year I work with people who simply won't, or can't, get it done. We know the process works, and we work very hard on the coaching. But sometimes there is a strong resistance. One of our clients called the resisting force within him "Mr. Perfectionist" and he allowed himself to waste months and months before he was ready to call the book "done".

Recently one of my clients admitted to faltering because of a lack of confidence around the concept, despite working it through to a really good level of detail. He was horrified to see another book come out with the exact title he was planning on using, and of course, you can't protect a title. There is a lot to be said for grabbing the first mover advantage and being the first to market with your idea, book, business, whatever. But this means you cannot allow yourself to go over and over the same idea, overthinking and overanalyzing things.

No brain dumps

There is a danger in writing everything down. What was a mess or a muddle in your head becomes a muddle on paper. It can be completely overwhelming and even paralyzing. I see aspiring authors who have created big beasts of mind maps, maps that are simply a brain dump. I ranted about brain dumping in *24 Carat BOLD*, but it is worth a reminder. I have never liked the imagery associated with the phrase. Do you? Is that something you would aspire to create? A brain dump? I didn't think so. Far more effective is a thoughtful process of allowing your best ideas to emerge, testing and tasting without committing to anything. It is essentially running your ideas through a small filter. Repeat the idea several times and ask yourself some key questions like:

- Is this what I really believe?
- Why do I believe this?
- Is it something that I want to be known for?

- Does it add value to people?
- If so, which people?

This doesn't have to be done in complete solitude. One of the ways to discover your best ideas and insights is via good coaching. Whether you go to a retreat or course, as described above, or whether you work with a coach or mentor on a one-to-one basis, you can get help, guidance and feedback on your thoughts and ideas. I'm very proud of this part of The Book Midwife® and REAL Thought Leaders methodology and process – drawing out the ideas through insightful questioning, testing, enhancing and refining of those ideas.

You do have wonderful, life-changing ideas

I occasionally use terms like life-changing with business audiences and there is always a mixed reaction. Many people don't see themselves as someone who changes lives. But what if you aren't seeing the impact you have on others, on the world? I think many of us underestimate the impact we can have, and do have. I give you permission to see it and be thankful for the way you have chosen to be, think and act up till now, which has already helped and inspired so many people.

The strapline of my publishing company, Panoma Press, is "books that change lives". I appreciate there are many other kinds of books and arguably there are some that don't change anyone's life. However, I am only interested in spending my precious time on this earth working with individuals who share my passion for developing themselves and others.

If I can only bring a few thousand books into the world during my lifetime, I choose to work with those that add tremendous value and create the massive shifts that are so sorely needed in our society today. Books that make people think. Books that encourage people to take action. Books that make people feel good about themselves and their contribution to the planet.

How about you? What kind of work are you committed to doing? What kind of leader are you committed to being?

Chapter 5
Positive Intention Leads to Positive Impact

"We are what we think. All that we are arises with our thoughts. With our thoughts, we make the world."

Buddha

You must find a way to get positive, and remain positive, for yourself and others. You also need to stay fresh and unsullied by ideas not in tune with your own.

Writing this book, I have been taking the advice that I give all my author clients: I am not reading any blogs, articles or books, nor watching any videos or having any conversations with others on this topic of carving out your own space. Unplug, unfollow, unfriend and even block if necessary. The most important thing is that you don't allow your own confidence and self-worth to falter, as you need to keep adding value and inspiring others.

Your self-worth allows you to create more and more value in the world, and other people can feel it. It's a tangible thing. It feeds everything else. It is the light in your eyes, and the energy that people feel when you interact with them. This is what needs to be protected. Your great feelings about and confidence in yourself and your special value. Everything else is secondary.

Marketing and promotion should be whatever you need and want it to be for your business and your brand. People will find you. Those folks that you are meant to work with will gravitate to you as a result of your sharing your best ideas, untainted and un-influenced by everything and everyone else.

Keep yourself pure – that's what I said to my friend, the one who was getting upset as she kept looking at what everyone else was doing. Pure means your own original, special uniqueness can shine through. Is it possible that it could sound "similar" to someone else's message? Of course it is. However, that should not stop you trying to create and deliver your best stuff.

Time to improve your thinking

There is a book called *Time to Think*, written by Nancy Kline, and an entire school of thought and material based on the book. I purposely haven't ever read the book, much as I was tempted to. But I felt I needed to practice what I preach, as described earlier in the book, and keep my own thinking "pure". I do intend to read the book at some point and find out more about Nancy's work and material, once my own book is in production and I am in no danger of copying any ideas. And I have a feeling there will be some synergies and perhaps even areas for collaboration. But for now, I am not looking at her material.

What I am interested in right now, and what I think all leaders could benefit from, is how we can come up with positive ideas fast. Because, let's face it, we are living in a fast-paced world where everything seems to come with a sense of urgency. How great would it be if you could tap into the best thinking anytime you needed to? Sometimes, it's as simple as going to look for it.

My son Bradley started a job last year which included organizing leaflet distribution in a shopping area. The goal was to get people to go to the shop, with a discount coupon. I asked if people were not wary of him or trying to avoid someone who approached them with a leaflet. I usually avoid people trying to hand me things as I walk down the street. Not always, but when I'm in a hurry, which sadly is most of the time, as it is with most people.

Brad explained that before he started the work, he searched for and found strategies online, which he adapted and refined on the job. He took time to think about how to approach people, what to say, and how to say it. Based on the research he had done, he even had a strategy for where to stand, how to react to questions and much more. All learned from videos on the Internet.

I admire people who think and plan, even a little, before jumping into something new. I am also impressed by the thought or idea to search for and find the answers there. I don't know if people in my generation (Baby Boomers) would even think to look online for this kind of information, or know what to search for!

How ingenious, to have the idea to learn a skill like that from watching videos. The Internet is an enabler and for the Millennials like Bradley, that is the first place they look – Google or, more likely, YouTube.

Starting out with the right intention can open up creative solutions for you too. Stopping to think for a moment longer than you normally would is not only possible but highly recommended. Taking even a few seconds to allow the best ideas to come is a way to honor the person with whom you are interacting. It shows you care.

You can learn how to care. Caring is all about intention, wanting the best for the other person, believing in them. Then, acting from that place of caring. People will definitely feel it, even if they are not able to articulate what it is about your communication that touches them. I have created an entire chapter about this later in the book, and I honestly think it is this kind of work that will give you the edge over people who are just churning out "stuff".

My most successful authors are usually the ones who really go for it in their communications. They wear their heart on their sleeve and let others get to know them. They think about the way the other person will receive their message, instead of trying to be clever.

I believe that strong-willed personality types need to let go of thinking of themselves in order to care about others. Being OK with yourself, your life and what value you add is a worthy goal. And as we have already seen, someone else's success does not take away from yours. As the Buddhist saying goes, the candle does not lose anything by lighting another candle.

This is the E in the REAL model: Engagement. It's the hardest one to grasp because although I called it a strategy, there is no real way of teaching it. I'm not sure there are many tangible ways of assessing engagement or caring. One that we work with a lot in my companies is language. The language you use when you speak with people one-to-one or speak to groups is critical. Your word choices can show you put real thought into your communication.

Writing has its challenges because the other person is not physically there to respond. This is why we spend extra time during our coaching and programs on key areas such as style, tone, intention and format of messages and content. So much can be misconstrued or misinterpreted, and if you are not there to explain yourself, you could miss the connection. Have you ever seen a discussion on social media get out of hand simply because of the way people interpreted the content? Aim to rise above that kind of communication, and put extra thought and care into everything you say, share and respond to online and offline. This attention alone will allow you to stand out.

> **Thought Bite:** Your word choices can show you put real thought into your communication @MindyGK

It is possible to create great engagement through writing. Just think of your own favorite authors and how you respond to their writing.

When I was doing the planning and writing sessions for this book, I worked from a place of caring about and sharing my best ideas with my ideal reader (hopefully you!). I obsessed with the way I put the ideas across and probably went against my own advice and did a bit too much thinking. But I would rather have it that way than not having thought about you enough.

Touching is another way to engage and show you care. My dad was always a touchy-feely kind of person. When he spoke with you, he really looked you in the eye, and he would often touch your arm to accentuate his meaning and create a deeper connection. He didn't just do this with family and close friends but with lots of people. I like to think I inherited Dad's tactile way of showing caring, but I think I may have toned it down a bit, during 20+ years of living in the UK. If you have met me, you will have to let me know if I am too touch-feely, not enough or just right!

Having said I toned my touchy-feely tendencies down to be more English, have you noticed that people in business are a lot more open to hugging and kissing than just five or ten years ago? I have seen people open up a lot more when speaking, writing and conversing, which is lovely. How are things where you are? Do you find people in business more open than five or ten years ago?

My good friend Tony Selimi, author of *A Path to Wisdom*, is a leading light in this area. The way he talks to his friends and contacts and even strangers is more intimate than most other leaders I have seen and met. Tony is always calling people "Lovely" and "Gorgeous", which makes you smile, even though you know he says it to everyone! He almost always ends his social media posts and emails by saying "I love you and thank you." He is always highlighting the good others are doing. Since everyone has a choice in how they interact with people, I often wonder how more people could do this, and what kind of impact it could have.

Woowoo Warning

Observe how you use the phrase "thank you" with your clients, suppliers, staff and others. Aim to say it more often by recognizing the good work people are doing. If you feel able to do it, introduce the words "love" or "I love you" in your communications. Now, I appreciate some people are not ready to receive these sorts of communications.

Remember from the earlier section how you can push your thinking, by focusing on something with a little extra time and attention? I know you can find a way to use the word "love" that will work for you and others. What I do quite often is sign emails "Love, Mindy" where appropriate. I think it surprises some people, but overall it creates really great engagement.

How the thoughtful leader uses their eyes

When you are in this thoughtful frame of mind, you will naturally look for ways to improve your communications and your actions. If you are coming from a conscious and intentional place, you will aim to achieve the right result for you and the other people involved. One of the exercises we do at my workshops involves looking someone in the eye while sharing different messages with them. When you meet people face-to-face, or even via Skype or Google+ or a similar video-based medium, you have a tremendous advantage. I always look right into my webcam when I'm the one speaking, as I know this will have the same effect on the person at the other end. Then, I look at them when they are speaking, and it makes a huge difference if they are looking into their webcam.

This is something the thoughtful leader can aspire to do whenever possible, to enhance eye contact and meaningful communications, in person and via video. This can be helpful when selling, helping clients, or dealing with a negative situation. In fact, the negative situation calls for special skills, and the thoughtful leader can turn things around better than most.

When you see something, say something

There can be real power in realizing you have hurt someone, and deciding to put it right. It takes courage, and it can be a humbling experience for both of you. After all, you are showing your vulnerability and imperfect character. And that opens a door for the other person to walk through.

A few months ago, I had a strange email from someone who had said he wanted to publish a book with us. It was someone I'd known and worked with years ago, but the tone was quite cold. I knew something was wrong and I didn't want to just leave the issue. It was scary to open up the conversation again, when the last communication had not been very friendly, but I felt I had to do it.

So I took a deep breath and asked if we could talk. I knew it was something bad and there were going to be some uncomfortable moments, but I wanted to be given the chance to respond differently. Sure enough, we had a conversation, and he revealed that I had not reacted to one of his ideas in a positive way. He made some assumptions and had decided that we were not going to move forward with any business. He would have left the issue there, and if I hadn't said anything, that would have been it. I wouldn't have known what the problem was. But I disrupted that thinking by opening up the conversation again, and he agreed to a meeting.

It's a question of looking for, and asking for, second chances. I do find myself doing this quite often, and I'm beginning to think it must be a hallmark of my leadership style. It seems tempting to "let sleeping dogs lie" but I can't do it.

Over 15 years ago, I was in a job interview situation. It was a telephone interview, there was no Skype at the time. I was listening hard, and trying to build rapport as well as I could, without eye contact or any other non-verbal clues. When the person interviewing me was winding up the call, he said something like, "OK, so we will be in touch." I knew I had not impressed him enough, and the opportunity was slipping away before my eyes.

So I opened my mouth and said something I think very few people would say. I said, "Wait. I feel I haven't impressed you enough and I'd like another chance." In other words, I said the exact thing I'd been sensing and thinking. To his credit, this guy said OK, we spent another ten or 15 minutes chatting, and the conversation ended with an invitation to attend an interview in person! I know for certain that I would not have achieved what I did on that telephone call had I not taken the risk and asked for what I wanted.

I can think of at least two or three other times in my life when I've used this strategy and it has worked. I can also recall times when it didn't work. But at least I tried. Not saying something would surely have closed down the opportunity completely. How could you begin to implement "see something, say something" philosophy? When could you start?

Chapter 6

How to Be a Centerpreneur

"Too often we... enjoy the comfort of opinion without the discomfort of thought."

John F. Kennedy

The thoughtful leader is a centered leader. You need to do whatever it takes to center yourself, and to approach life in a grounded way. Let's talk about these two words for a moment.

First, let's consider the word centered. The word is generally understood by many people, but what does it actually mean? I believe it speaks of the fact that you are either at the center of your life, or you are moving restlessly around the edges. If you are, or have had times in life where you were, moving restlessly around the edges, you probably experienced anxiety and uncertainty. One of the basic human needs is certainty or security; therefore, a feeling of uncertainty means that need is not being met. Even if you like the idea of spontaneity, changing situations and variety, you still need to know who you are and where you are in life.

> **Thought Bite:** You are either at the center of your life, or you are moving restlessly around the edges @MindyGK

Picture a pond where a stone has just been thrown into the water. At the exact spot where the stone hit the water, the indentation is deeper than anywhere else. As the ripples begin to spread out, the depth of each ripple is slightly less than the one closer to the center.

Life and relationships work in the same way. The people closest to you get to know you the best; they see the "real" you. Allowing people close to you is a choice, and you may choose not to do it. Perhaps you don't feel it is your style, or personality type. I am not saying that everyone needs to wear their heart on their sleeve, but when you do, magical things start to happen.

When you are centered, others can feel more centered

For a leader, this need for certainty is even more important. By definition, a leader has followers, people who look up to them. Those people are also looking for certainty. They may rely on and trust that leader's opinions and actions. They are looking for guidance and direction. The first step is to center yourself, so that you can hold a stable place in others' perception of you. And this definitely spills over to their perception of your business, if you are the leader of the business.

Being grounded is similar, but the key aspect is the relationship with the ground or the earth. Imagine a large bunch of helium-filled balloons. Those balloons are going to float up into the sky, unless they are held together and tethered to a weight of some kind. You may have seen balloons attached to weights at special events like weddings and product launches. Keeping the balloons on the ground, or keeping your feet on the ground, is essential.

How to find your center

You may have noticed that personal development has exploded over the past ten years or so. At my publishing company, we have seen a huge uptake in sales of our personal development or self-help books. I believe this is because we are in a new age, where people are not content to live a two-dimensional life any longer. The materialism and cut-and-thrust of the 80s and 90s is behind us, and people seem to want more from life now. Even if you are in your dream job or running your ideal business, you may occasionally feel like you need to nurture the other areas of your life. So, the search for balance is normal.

Get coaching

You must have heard of coaching. I'm not talking about sports coaching, but rather life coaching, executive coaching, and business coaching. You may have even enlisted the help of various coaches in your life and business. Coaching is really valuable, in terms of getting clarity and direction around what is important to you, how you want to show up as a leader and as a person, and even how to achieve key outcomes in your life and business. I have been in the coaching world for 13 years now, and it never ceases to amaze me how much progress people can make when they are willing to look into their lives and decisions, ask for help and push beyond the easy answers.

All thoughtful leaders are willing to examine their lives and look to improve themselves continually. Some folks think coaching is all about fixing problems, and it can be used for that. However, the leaders who work on themselves regularly keep themselves centered and grounded, which means they are better equipped to handle problems as they arise, and tend to handle them with more grace and ease. So, rather than viewing coaching as a quick fix or a Band-Aid, you may want to view it as an ongoing mental and emotional conditioning tool, one that strengthens your core more and more.

You're grounded!

In the U.S., where I grew up, the biggest punishment you could inflict on a teenager was to "ground" them. This means not being allowed to leave the house to do anything fun. Obviously you had to go to school and any important educational activities, but nothing social. If you got grounded at the wrong time, you could miss parties, sports events, concerts or even Halloween. Yes, yours truly was very naughty in the week leading up to Halloween, and missing the trick-or-treating was deemed to be an appropriate punishment. I thought they were going to relent just at the last minute, but no, my sister was allowed to go out and I had to stay home and answer the door to all the other little kids. I'm still scarred for life! (Not really.)

Being grounded can be a positive thing, though. The other meaning, of course, is that you have your feet on the ground, implying that you are stable or solid. This is a valuable trait in an age where fewer people commit to jobs and relationships for the long term. People in your work life, and in your personal life, still crave certainty or stability, and if you can give that to them, they will love you.

Centering yourself is an essential step in the entrepreneurial process

As I have already shown, entrepreneurship is more accessible and easier than ever, but that can have its drawbacks as well. It is so easy to start a business, and it involves so much less risk than ever before, that people often don't put the time in up front to really think things through. Typically they don't do much in terms of planning the business properly, nor do they consider the implications on other aspects of their lives, such as family, finances or social life. They just jump in.

The entrepreneur can be the worst at planning because he feels he is the "idea guy". He doesn't want to get bogged down in boring things like planning. He wants to jump on the idea now. See it online tomorrow. Generate incredible results overnight. That's the exciting part of the dream. The planning bit is not. Is this resonating with you? If so, you probably have the spirit of an entrepreneur!

However, I have seen it over and over again in the entrepreneurs I have been privileged to meet and work with. The ones who rush in often have to deal with issues and problems later on. But leaders who don't act quickly enough often miss the mark with their market because they appear to be wavering and not truly committed.

How to stay centered with multiple hats on or multiple plates spinning

Do you run several businesses? It's hard to split the time sensibly. And what about your business cards? Do you have more than one? Is it like in *Hello Dolly!* where Dolly Levi shows up at an event and offers people a choice of cards? "Pick a card, any card" may be fun and you may feel that it keeps your options open, but it does not give a lot of confidence to your market, or specifically to someone looking to spend money with you. As you may know, people really prefer to work with experts or specialists, not generalists.

But it's not just about the practicalities of splitting your time or deciding which marketing materials to take to a meeting. Far more challenging is the feeling of having a "split personality", where you find it difficult to know who or what you are anymore. Or the issue of your different responsibilities competing with each other or cannibalizing each other.

I believe the answer lies in finding the one thread that ties your multiple businesses or interests together. So, in addition to planning and working on the various projects, you also need to plan and clarify your "big picture" or map. This will give you a great sense of relief and clarity to make decisions and communicate with others.

Would you ever start a long and important journey without a map (or GPS or a map app)?

Last year, I had a private client who showed up to start planning a business book. However, it soon became apparent, through the coaching questions, that the big picture was not clear. We immediately parked the book discussion and turned our attention to where he was trying to take his business and what specific outcomes he had for that business, and for his life. He thought he was there to work on a book (and he was, and we did) but we first needed to get the map sorted out, then it was much easier to see how the book fit into that.

We find ourselves doing this quite a bit with clients. It is the best ones who admit they need to work on their vision or strategy before diving into the job of creating content. Being open, honest and transparent pays huge dividends, the greatest one being that you can create a much more powerful and effective thought leadership strategy.

> **Thought Bite:** Thoughtful leaders carve out the time to be thoughtful @MindyGK

See if you can generate a few statements about yourself, your life and your priorities that hold true no matter what business or aspect of your life you are discussing. I would recommend deep exploration of your core values and beliefs, as well as your goals and preferences. Personality profile or similar work may also be beneficial at this stage. If you need or want help with this, I do some of this kind of work, but I also have other very talented coaches and consultants in my network who specialize in exactly this. So just ask me.

Then, as with the other ideas in this book, once you learn how to do this work for yourself, it is time to share it with others in your network, organization or community. Sharing it reinforces it for you, helps you articulate your thinking, and helps others to create the same benefits for themselves. Don't be selfish with this! The more people you can engage with at this level, the more rewarding you will find your work, and your life.

> **Thought Bite:** In addition to planning and working on the various projects, you also need to plan and clarify your "big picture" @MindyGK

This work on yourself is not something to be done once and then forgotten about. As you are going to continually change and evolve as a person, you want to ensure that your life plan and your life itself continue to make sense and make you happy.

My best advice is to schedule time to go through important personal goals, outcomes and vision, not just once a year, like New Year's resolution time, but regularly – say, once a quarter. Thoughtful leaders carve out the time to be thoughtful.

Chapter 7

Making Milestones Matter

"The safest road to hell is the gradual one - the gentle slope, soft underfoot, without sudden turnings, without milestones, without signposts."

C.S. Lewis

Milestones are all around us, and they can be a motivating force that pulls you forward or a debilitating force that holds you back. The choice of how to perceive them is yours, and ironically it depends on your ability to live life in the moment and seize and celebrate as often as you can, as powerfully as you can. The thoughtful leader uses milestones proactively and positively.

I celebrate every milestone in a big way. I held parties to remember for my 30th, 40th and 50th birthdays. And my 29th, my 42nd and many others!

You want to use the milestone as a catalyst or a deadline. Deadline is a horrible word though. How about the phrase we use in our companies: target dates?

Milestones or millstones?

Milestones will occur whether you mark them or not. It's all about your attitude.

It does help create focus when there is a date or impending event or milestone staring you in the face. Some people ignore birthdays and don't make a big deal about key dates. Some people I know get agitated thinking about getting older, like a millstone hanging around their neck, dragging them down. So for them, pushing it under the rug is a form of denial.

I don't want to make my milestone-averse friends wrong, but I really think key dates and anniversaries help to punctuate your life. Tradition! As Tevye said in *Fiddler on the Roof*. We need traditions, customs, rituals. Acknowledging these milestones cements their importance in your mind and creates energy.

> **Thought Bite:** Milestones will occur whether you mark them or not
> @MindyGK

Energy in turn creates thoughts, or, as some people would say, thoughts *are* energy. You want to come up with some great ideas? You want to be more creative? Focus on the target and celebrate everything you can, as often as you can.

When The Book Midwife® was reaching ten years in business, I began to plan a party. However, as the date approached, we were not having the best financial quarter, and I went back and forth several times about whether the party should go ahead. In the end, I decided we absolutely had to have a celebration with as many of our authors and extended community as possible. After all, you only turn ten once! With a bit of creativity and ingenuity, we managed to hold a fantastic party without breaking the bank. It was so important to my staff and our clients, and it gave everybody a big lift.

By the time this book is in print, Panoma Press will also be reaching its tenth birthday, and we will definitely be celebrating that – big time. I hope you are part of the celebration!

How a major milestone became my hot button

One key milestone which no one enjoys talking about or hearing about is the menopause. Sorry, I've gone and said it now! I don't mind admitting my age or the fact that my body started betraying me earlier this year. At least, that's how I saw it at first, as I sat there with my hot flashes, resenting the fact I couldn't control them. Then I had the most amazing thought: this is my time! Some people will recognize that phrase as part of a euphemism for menopause: time of life. Now, *that* is a silly phrase because every stage is a time of life! But I digress.

So there I was with my hot flashes, and I began using them to feel empowered and lucky. I mean, how lucky am I to be nice and warm in what can be a cold and damp climate?! Not only that, but my moments tend to wake me up in the wee hours of the morning, as blood courses through my body, suffusing my face and neck. I can feel the blood in my head and I choose to have that mean my brain is being fed with oxygen. Whatever the physiological truth about it all (and don't even bother to tell me) I have created my own meaning. When it happens now, I wake up cheerfully and begin exploring creative ideas. You may be interested to know that this book only started progressing in earnest because of these "moments".

I bet you are now wishing it was your time of life. Well, guess what: it is! No matter what your age or even if you are a man, you can create your own moments to sit or lie quietly, or walk in nature, and be creative. Let your best thoughts and ideas flow, because you can.

Exercise:

Identify the next five milestones in your life and business. Give each one a "gut feel score" in terms of how happy or excited you are about it. Now think about how you could make the event more meaningful and more exciting, for you and others. Think of something you could do to mark the occasion or celebrate. Write it down – just a word or two will do for now, to capture the idea.

Milestone	Happy score	How to Celebrate

Thought Bite: Let your best thoughts and ideas flow, because you can
@MindyGK

Acknowledge and celebrate others' milestones

When my husband Phil and I got married, we merged our last names, and we also merged certain other things in our lives. Such as the family birthday calendar. For the most part, after 21 years of being together, we still maintain the responsibility of remembering our own original family members' key dates. But life has become busier for everyone, and we often travel out of town or out of the country. It can take extra effort to remember to buy the card, write a message, address it and mail it.

We have other means at our fingertips now as well. There are birthday apps and Facebook reminders. I even have one of the apps on my phone, to ensure that the birthdays show up in my calendar. But if you want to do something special and send a real card, you can't wait until the reminder on the day itself.

> **Exercise:**
>
> Write down a few things that you could do to show appreciation for different people in your life. Really dig deep and be creative. You will be giving a gift to yourself as well as the other person.
>
> **Family members**
>
> **Friends**
>
> **Staff**
>
> **Customers and clients**

I must have several dozen suppliers that I use, in life and in business, and yet only a handful of them remember my birthday at all. In some cases, I get an SMS text message on my phone, perhaps with a special offer in honor of the day – ten percent off a haircut or something similar.

What are you doing for your clients or customers? Do you know their key dates, such as birthdays and anniversaries? People will feel more trust and more loyalty toward those leaders who take the time – and extra thought and care – to remember and acknowledge important events in their customers' lives.

Be creative

Earlier, I said celebrate everything you can, as often as you can. One of our authors, Bryony Thomas, is a complete inspiration in this area. When her book *Watertight Marketing* was first launched, she felt unable to hold a launch party because she had just lost her father to cancer. So, when the first anniversary of the book rolled around, Bryony decided to have a combined party for the launch and the one-year anniversary of the book. It was a huge success, with hundreds of colleagues, clients and friends, great atmosphere, professional delivery and fun. Bryony has just had the second anniversary of the book's launch, and she says she intends to hold a Book Birthday Party every year!

What could you celebrate, if you got really creative? Just about anything, I imagine. Look for more opportunities to make a big party out of some good news.

Thought Bite: This is your time of life
@MindyGK

Chapter 8

The Thoughtful Leader Takes Risks Thoughtfully

"The risk of a wrong decision is preferable to the terror of indecision."

Maimonides

Your risk profile

It is important to acknowledge how you behave as a leader, in terms of your approach to risk. Do you know how you perceive risk, and how you operate with regard to risk, in different areas of your life?

I was lucky enough to have had my risk profile assessed with a tool called Navitas Risk Indicator, by global coaching firm Shirlaws. It goes through lots of areas where you make decisions, and rates your risk tendency for each area. Most importantly, it gives you a starting point to understand your behavior as it pertains to risk, and the results of your likely decision-making. I think this kind of tool is essential for leaders, especially thoughtful leaders who want to be more and do more. If you want to learn more about the Navitas Risk Indicator, simply go to their website: www.navitasip.com

So what do you do with the information? You can look to shift your thinking and behavior slightly, but I wouldn't spend a lot of time on that. I would, instead, work with your tendencies and turn them into even greater strengths.

You probably need, and hopefully have, people around you who complement your skills and experience. What about people who complement your approach to risk? Sometimes, when you need to make big decisions, that alternative view can be critical. I have a fairly high risk profile, in most things. Therefore I have found slightly more risk-averse business partners, mentors and advisers are the best people to surround myself with. They ensure that I don't jump in too fast without considering options and consequences.

In addition, I have also learned to insert more time to reflect, compared to my early years in business. Partly this new behavior came from making mistakes and learning from those mistakes; I have also observed other leaders over my many years in business, and I have aimed to model their best traits.

> **Thought Bite:** Sometimes, when you need to make big decisions, that alternative view can be critical @MindyGK

Risk takers are good leaders

Paralysis by analysis is not generally effective because leadership decisions often need to be made swiftly. Read any book on leadership and the idea of risk-taking and decision-making is mentioned. Just think about leaders that you admire and ask yourself if they take risks and make big decisions. Now, ask yourself that most difficult question of all:

What risk do you need to take that would create the biggest shift for you right now?

The thoughtful risk-taker

Whether you have a high or low risk profile, if you want to be an effective leader, you will need to pause for thought but not deliberate for too long. I wish I could give you a specific number of seconds, minutes, hours or days you should take contemplating options, or a clever formula to follow, but I'm sure you can see that decision-making is too complex to be turned into a precise equation.

Every day, I seem to be encouraging my clients to take more risks with their writing. We have already discussed the perils of putting out bland content that doesn't add value. It will waste your time and others' time. It will make people think you don't have anything original to say. By now, you may have been inspired by some of the bold claims and examples I have included in this book. You may be thinking that it's time for you to shake things up, to set your wildest idea into motion, to really go for it. That's great and I applaud you, but before you take that flying leap, just read the next section and reflect for a few moments.

Don't take stupid risks

Before we go any further, I want to make sure we are on the same page regarding the context for this section. We have been looking at improving thought processes, so that you can go to market with ideas that have been thought through properly. We have started to talk about important leadership qualities, one of which is the ability to take sensible risks and decide on key issues that affect the business.

So the phrase I want you to bear in mind is "sensible risks". Nobody will be impressed if you bet the company's profits on a day trade, or get into a business relationship with a stranger that you haven't researched in any way. (Both of these are real examples of risks people in my network took over the past six months.)

> **Thought Bite:** Go to market with ideas that have been thought through properly @MindyGK

I choose to use the phrase "sensible risk" instead of the more common "calculated risk" because the calculation bit can be a little too tempting for those wanting to defer the decision by doing too much analysis. In other words, we don't need you to calculate, but rather to use your common sense.

Chapter 9

Being Truly Thoughtful – Baring, Sharing and Daring to Care

"Caring about others, running the risk of feeling, and leaving an impact on people, brings happiness."

Harold Kushner

Being truly thoughtful is not only a nice thing to aspire to; it can create wealth and abundance in your personal life and business. You just need to care enough to want to do it, and to try new strategies, if what you have done in the past has not worked well enough.

I have put my best ideas into this chapter and it may still be challenging for some people. Leadership has been expressed in so many different ways in other books and articles that it is not my intention to reinvent the wheel. I just want to focus on how you conduct yourself, in life and in business, and see if there is an opportunity for you to create a small shift in your thinking and behavior, which could lead to a big shift in results.

You have probably seen this next quotation before, but it is so perfect for this section that I just had to include it here, even though you have already had one inspirational quotation for this chapter.

> *"Never doubt that a small group of thoughtful, committed citizens could change the world. Indeed, it is the only thing that ever has."*
> **Margaret Mead**

The narcissistic, materialistic and egotistical ways of the twentieth century are passé. Finished. Obsolete. Of course, you may still see some people in your industry or community behaving like they are living in the last century. As I have stated, they may be operating from a place of fear, lack and scarcity. The thoughtful leader understands that the only way to true success and fulfillment is to engage with others in a more open and caring way. We now get to explore the other side of the thoughtful coin.

Being thoughtful is not the same as being kind

Being kind is one of the ways to be thoughtful. However, it is not always appropriate, and you can easily misuse kindness in business situations. For example, you may be leading a team or a member of a team, and someone is not pulling their weight. They are trying really hard but they just aren't cutting it. You don't want to bring it up because, well, it's not really a big issue and you don't want to cause this team member any more anxiety, and anyway you are getting results despite this person's incompetence. You don't want to be unkind. But, in fact, not saying something, not confronting the issue is being unkind and unfair to the other person.

Sometimes, as the song goes, "you gotta be cruel to be kind."

(**"Cruel to Be Kind"** is a 1979 single written by Nick Lowe and his former Brinsley Schwarz bandmate Ian Gomm)

In coaching terms, this is often called "tough love". If you don't like the word "love" in a business context, get over yourself. It is becoming more and more widely accepted, and the leaders who really understand how to love and show love – yes, even in business – are the ones who will be moving ahead in the new business model.

I honestly believe that, at their core, most people do want to be loving and caring. They simply revert to deep-seated fears and fight or flight instincts when they perceive things are not going well. Note that I say "they perceive". They panic and begin to focus on themselves and their own challenges. They ignore or don't even bother to concern themselves with other people's problems. There simply isn't any space left in their worried, fretting mind for anything other than their own stuff.

If you have found yourself in this state in the past, recently, or even currently, relax. Smile and know that you are not a bad person. Really! You just get a little bit preoccupied with stuff, live in your head a bit and forget that there are ways to manage things.

There are tools to help you remember others. As I mentioned, we have all the birthday apps. Before Facebook alerted me and reminded me about people's birthdays, I probably didn't even know when most of my contacts' birthdays were. Now, I have the opportunity to see thousands of birthday notifications, so I don't forget to send my wishes to that person. You have probably seen nice posts from people you know, one day after their birthday, thanking the many well-wishers.

Posting on someone's wall is certainly an efficient way of showing you care. Creating a private message goes one step further, as it takes a little effort. I count a text or personal email as even more caring. And a phone call, which requires even more time and thought, is even better. But the old-fashioned hard-copy birthday card trumps them all. We all know that takes time, effort and a little money to buy the card, handwrite it, address it and send it in the mail.

These days, when everything seems to be "one click for ease", taking the extra time to do something special stands out. I try (but do not always manage) to make the extra effort, not just to be seen to be doing it but because I know how I would feel if I were the recipient.

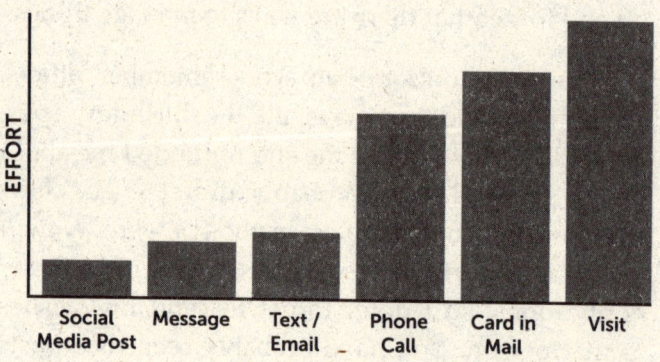

The thoughtful leader spends time really thinking about someone else's needs. They put the other person's needs first, in some cases making sacrifices.

It's easy to do this with loved ones, but this concept applies to all relationships. In business, this has been described as win-win. Who wouldn't want a win-win outcome, given the choice? It sounds, and is, much nicer than win-lose. This area is explored really well in the negotiation strategies taught by my friend Chris Merrington. Learning how to look at all situations in this way, not just business and not just negotiation, could give you a great advantage in life.

Being thoughtful can be a way of life.

Random acts of kindness are worth doing every day. They improve your chemical state by releasing the feel-good hormones. Several bloggers I follow, including Bridget Hunt, author of the excellent book *Six Pack Chick*, recommend doing random acts of kindness, where you do something kind for someone, sometimes without even telling them. You may know, if you have practiced this in the past, that it's not only the recipient of the random act that benefits. The feel-good hormones kick in for the giver when doing these things.

Bridget did a month-long initiative last year where she challenged herself and others to do these random acts of kindness and post publicly about the random acts and the results.

The more you see things this way, the more you will act in this way, and you will develop the habit of being thoughtful.

Think before you speak

There have been times in my life when I said something I regretted, and wished the earth would open up and swallow me whole. Perhaps you have had situations like that too? I'm pleased to say that as I've got older (matured?), those situations have become rarer, and I attribute that to taking a bit more time, a bit more of a pause before I speak.

Not too much, mind you. In this fast-paced world of today, if you always hesitate, or take too much time to ponder situations, replies and the like, things can shift very fast and you may miss out.

Personal development literature refers to a 25 millisecond pause between action and reaction. That means there is a split-second of opportunity that we can learn to notice and use to our advantage, so we don't always have to react so quickly. Or say things we will later regret.

A generous member of my mastermind group, Barnaby Wynter, is an exceptional example of someone who thinks before speaking, then comes up with really great insights. He tends to sit quietly when others are speaking, a pensive look on his face, rarely the first to comment. Then he shares the most amazing and accurate insights. Barnaby doesn't mince his words, and he doesn't hold back from some tough love advice, which absolutely comes from his heart.

But the action that stands out the most for me is a phone conversation we were having, where the moment I expressed a challenge I was having in my business, he insisted we spend the majority of the call absolutely obsessed with helping me resolve that issue. He wasn't thinking about when we would turn the conversation around to him and his business. He just wanted to help because that's what thoughtful leaders do.

Could you look for more opportunities to help? Not just respond or react, but actively seek out these opportunities? It could be that once you turn on the radar, more and more chances will appear.

I noticed several years ago that an entrepreneur in my network always seemed to be in the right place at the right time to help people. Maksoom Hussain is a property investor and landlord who posts very openly on Facebook about property and a whole lot more. Maksoom is actually a leader in the area of kindness, as she always has a story to share and inspire others. She consistently does things like noticing people who are in trouble, or simply people who are doing great things and should be recognized. The reason why Maksoom's stories stand out is that this type of behavior (or at least posting online about it) is rare.

Maksoom's generous pay-it-forward mentality has already begun to have ripple effects. I found myself on a train with a Chinese woman whose husband had accidentally stepped off the train at the wrong stop. She and I were still on the train and she was panicking. In halting English, she explained they were visiting from overseas. Her husband had a mobile phone he'd borrowed from the relatives they were staying with, but she didn't know the number. She didn't know how to reach him, and she didn't know how she was going to get back to the station where he had got off the train.

Within moments, a question popped into my head: "What would Maksoom do?" I immediately knew the answer and reassured the woman, as we left at my station, and I walked her over to the other platform to catch another train. I wanted to get on that train with her, in case there were problems, but she assured me she could figure it out from there. So I did the next best thing and gave her my card and asked if she could email or text me when she was reunited with her husband. I got an email an hour later from a very grateful lady.

Was it hard to do what I did? No. Did it cost me anything? Only about two minutes of my time and a little anxiety, until I heard back from her. But most people didn't do anything, and in many situations (if I were rushed or stressed or had my head down, looking at my phone) I might not have done anything either. Instead, a very thoughtful leader called Maksoom had shown me another possibility. Who could you be inspired by? Better yet, what could you do right now to become a more thoughtful leader and inspire others?

Think before you write

Although I covered this topic in great depth in *24 Carat BOLD*, I just wanted to reiterate the main points for you here. There are many ways to get your message across in writing these days: books, ebooks, articles, blogs, social media posts, newsletters, emails... No matter what the medium, every time you write, you have the chance to influence and inspire – or not. To make a relevant and important point – or not. Remember the offer of the gym membership by the folks who want to sell houses. Make sure you really think things through before putting stuff out there.

Looking back and reflecting

So often, I see business leaders flying around from one meeting, conference, event or conversation to the next. The "too busy, too busy" state that many people find themselves in is counterproductive and even dangerous. It is crucial to capture the ideas, learnings, actions and decisions immediately after an important meeting or event.

A colleague recently told me about the meetings policy at his workplace, where meetings are 50 minutes in length instead of one hour, to give people time to reflect, write any extra notes and get to the next meeting. How clever! If you have back-to-back meetings, logistics become a challenge. You can't go over your allotted time, not even by a minute, without being late for the next appointment. Even telephone calls with no travel time in between can be stressful. I mean, you might need to grab a drink or deal with a call of nature!

> **Thought Bite:** The "too busy, too busy" state that many people find themselves in is counterproductive and even dangerous @MindyGK

How can you create more time in your busy schedule for reflection and processing ideas?

How to apologize thoughtfully

When you start to think and reflect more, you will find yourself becoming thoughtful about your actions, sometimes with regret. No matter how much thought you put into your words and actions, it is inevitable that you will occasionally say and do things you wish you hadn't. It's called being human!

In Chapter 5, I introduced the idea of saying something to improve a situation. Now I want to show you exactly how you can use this strategy for yourself and create miracles in your own life.

Firstly, instead of calling the behavior "bad" or "negative", I prefer to use the term "unresourceful". We all have certain resources available to us, such as caring, kindness, intelligence etc. It's just that sometimes we forget we have them, and forget to use them. We act or speak unresourcefully.

The key is what you do about it, how you deal with it and how fast. I'm sure you know that the longer a negative feeling goes on, in your mind or someone else's, the more it has time to fester, grow or even transform into something really ugly.

Catching yourself is more than half the battle. Self-aware leaders can be and act in the moment, while seeing themselves at the same time and sometimes seeing it all from the other person's point of view. It is like shooting a film with two cameras and acting in it at the same time!

Trust me, you can get better at this. You can get really good, to the point that you can stop yourself mid-sent…

Oh, come on, you've got to have fun with this stuff. Laugh at yourself. When you do, others relax and the whole relationship moves to one that is more comfortable and positive.

Become a Mr. Fix It (or Ms. Fix It)

Now let's talk about what to do for those times you don't manage to catch yourself until the dirty deed is done or the sentence you didn't mean to utter is out of your mouth. Remember, the key is speed, so you don't want to agonize over it for days, weeks and months. You have a chance to impress the other person with your grace and fluidity.

When it happens, as fast as you can, write down two things that you would say to fix things. I encourage you to write down two things and not just one, since you will be giving yourself back some power of choice. You chose to do or say whatever it was at the time; now you can choose between two positive options, so it's going to be a win-win whatever happens!

Then, if the person is still there in front of you or on the telephone, take a short, deep breath, pick one of your fix-it lines and say it sincerely. There is magic in this stuff. You will feel great during and after. You can't control how the other person will respond, but nine times out of ten, they will be very happy and forgive you.

If you have done something you need to resolve with action, write down two actions you could take, then pick one and find a way to do it – fast.

So, in summary, you need to catch yourself saying, thinking or doing those unresourceful things. Then you need to think fast and act – fast.

Chapter 10

You Can Learn to Care

*"Too often we underestimate the power of
a touch, a smile, a kind word, a listening ear,
an honest compliment, or the smallest act of caring, all of
which have the potential to
turn a life around."*
Leo Buscaglia

Caring is a human trait but some people have allowed other emotions to bury their caring nature. It is something that is almost certainly learned, or which lies dormant for the first few years of life. I think you would agree that the only person a baby really cares about is itself! Getting its own needs met is a full-time preoccupation, and it learns what caring is and how to do it only through observing other people, and in some cases overt teaching by a parent, teacher or religious leader.

I must say, I had mixed feelings about including this chapter. Firstly, who am I to teach people how to care? Am I always the perfect example of a caring individual? No. Far from it. I have, at times, forgotten friends and family members' birthdays, not made an effort to call people often enough, wallowed in my own concerns and problems, shut myself off from outside help and thrown charity leaflets in the trash. And I'm sure I have forgotten many other crimes of selfishness or omission!

However, I thought the concept important enough to include in the book, and I can offer my own perspective on things. Since I am on my own continuous journey, I am still "consciously incompetent" at some of these things, but I would like to think I am much better than I was, and I think I am coming from the right place.

If you keep your eyes open, there are lots of good examples in your life of people you can learn from. Jacquie is a good friend of mine who has had her fair share of challenges over the years. Health issues, marital issues, financial concerns – you name it, she has been through it. However, despite everything, she always makes time to think of others, ask after them, remember birthdays and provide cheerful support and encouragement for people in her life.

Choosing to care

Caring requires you to be emotionally available and open. But sometimes we don't feel like being open. It's easier to keep things to ourselves. That's OK sometimes, but every time you say "I don't care" about anything or anyone, you distance yourself from the issue and from other people who do care about that issue and close off opportunities.

It can also look like laziness when you don't even offer an opinion. It is rather lazy and kind of mean to ignore things that are important to people who are important to you. Imagine if you opened up about a topic that was close to your heart, and others couldn't be bothered to pay attention or comment. Maybe that has happened to you already.

I'm not saying you need to care about every single thing, but caring enough to give this issue a little thought, and caring enough to let people know what you think, can create the open channel of communication I was speaking of earlier.

Even if people don't agree with you (and it's OK and even desirable to have differing opinions from others), by taking the time to decide how you feel, and voicing your thoughts, you show respect for the person who initiated the conversation.

Try this on social media. The next time someone close to you posts an update or asks a question about something you are not really interested in, spend just five seconds thinking about whether you *could* care one way or the other. And if you did, how would you feel about that issue or situation? Then decide if you want to declare your position. You don't have to comment; as I've said earlier, it's just good to push your thinking a bit.

The Law of Attraction states that what you focus on expands and you begin to attract more of it into your life. Therefore, focusing on caring and making it a key part of who you are will help that part of you to grow.

How to become a more caring person

The first thing you need to do is be aware of your current state and emotions. Are you stressed? Worried about things? Angry? Those are all states that make it very difficult to think about others, as you are focusing inward and on your own problems. Many years ago, I practiced meditation and found it very helpful for clearing my mind of all the thoughts and craziness, and having a little inner peace. Meditation is well known for creating a calmer state, and it is from this state that you will be more effective at many activities, but especially thinking of others.

One of the meditations I was fortunate to learn was called the Metta Bhavana, which is all about loving kindness. It helped me focus on caring about my welfare and that of others in my life. It even extends to people you don't know, and the world at large. I highly recommend doing something like this to put yourself into a loving and caring frame of mind. There are many courses, apps, downloads and other resources available to guide you through it.

Write down your goals around caring

Before you even start, you will want to set some outcomes for your caring. This might seem strange – to have goals about caring. But if it is something you want to work on and improve, you need to approach it in exactly the same way as anything else you want to achieve in life.

If you know how to articulate goals in a SMART way (Specific, Measurable, Attainable, Relevant and Time-Bounded) then use that method. Otherwise, simply write down a few statements that show how you would like your behavior to be in the future. Give yourself some ways of measuring the result; for example, noticing that people say thank you more often, as a result of your caring and acting in a more thoughtful way.

Watch your words

Watch the words you use on a daily basis, especially about others. It is amazing what a high percentage of the thoughts we have and words we use are negative. We have tens of thousands of thoughts every day, and according to various sources, between 80 percent and 95 percent of them are negative!

You probably grew up hearing some kind of advice like "If you can't say something nice, don't say anything at all." These words have some truth in them! Surely you don't want to be known as someone who constantly criticizes others or finds fault with them. You can aspire to be that person everyone looks up to as a "really good person".

Be extra careful when committing words to paper or the Internet. The Internet can have a long memory, and a cache where all kinds of silly impetuous statements are stored. If you do write something while you are highly emotional, save it and sleep on it overnight. In the morning, with a clearer head, you may choose to modify the wording or the tone of your message.

> **Thought Bite:** You can aspire to be that person everyone looks up to as a "really good person" @MindyGK

Look out for opportunities to care more

What do I mean by "care more"? Well, I mean you can care more than you would have, if you had not been focused on it. I also mean caring more than the average person does. It does take extra effort, but that effort is always rewarded. I first heard the following quotation over 25 years ago, and it still rings true for me and guides me in my work:

"There are no traffic jams on the extra mile."

Zig Ziglar

Fantastic concept, isn't it? Since so many people are unwilling to put in that extra effort, to go that extra mile, the people who do really stand out. When do you have an opportunity to go the extra mile and care more than you normally do, or more than the person next to you? Here are some examples to start you off:

- When your team member or staff member is noticeably upset about something but hasn't said anything

- When you are supposed to be having a short meeting, but the person you are meeting with shares something personal and important to them

- When you have a tight deadline and a family member or close friend needs you

- When someone answers your "How are you?" with "I'm fine" but they obviously are not fine

- When someone you know has been attacked or bullied online, and you feel outraged

Of course, in all of these situations, and many others I'm sure you will encounter, you have the choice to leave things unsaid, to do the bare minimum, to get on with your busy life. After all, it requires that extra time and effort. It requires you to stick your neck out. The thoughtful leader goes beyond the obvious, beyond the call of duty, and sticks their neck out as often as possible. The thoughtful leader cares enough to show others how much they care.

Chapter 11

Think Bigger

"As long as you're going to be thinking anyway, think big."

Donald Trump

Whatever vision you have for yourself, your company, your business or the world, you could probably expand it. It doesn't take much more effort to play a bigger game and to have a greater vision. If you don't think bigger, who will? Don't leave it for someone else to do because it may not get done.

To think bigger, you have to be bigger

I don't mean physically, of course. I'm talking about being a bigger person, being the best person you can be. Playing small is an acceptable strategy for the average person. They know that playing bigger and thinking bigger takes a little extra effort, and they are not willing to push themselves and make that effort. But you aren't average. I know this because you picked up this book and you have nearly made it to the end.

Being the bigger person also has connotations of being magnanimous, forgiving others, practicing a higher level of thinking. This takes effort, but it also takes courage and inner strength. Sometimes you have to admit you were wrong. Or you have to look for peaceful resolutions even when you know the other person was wrong. If you have the chance to expand your influence and impact, but you are stuck in pettiness and inner turmoil, it is likely you won't act. Then someone else may be the hero, or, more likely, no one will act and the situation will remain unresolved.

You can't worry about how you will look; you act from a place of knowing what is right and caring about the outcome. Where could you make a difference today, if you just let go of a negative emotion? Please note that I don't actually believe emotions are "negative" or "positive" as they are all valuable; I am just using this terminology for ease of understanding.

You can't even begin to think properly if your mind is mired in negative emotions such as hatred, spite, jealousy and revenge. The bigger person finds a way to come to terms with these emotions and move on to a cleaner inner state. Then the exciting work can begin.

Bigger and more often

If you want to do this stuff properly, you may need to commit to a few new habits. As I suggested earlier, you may want to set aside a little time each day or a few times a week, to focus on the important ideas without getting distracted by trivial things. With the speed of new ideas entering the market, it is hard to know whether innovation has got faster, or it's just that ideas spread so fast nowadays. Or maybe it's both.

One thing is certain: thinking big has never been more essential, and this trend will not be going away anytime soon. Thoughtful leaders have more big thoughts, and more often. It is the thoughtful leaders who will lead the way into the next wave.

> **Thought Bite:** Thinking big has never been more essential @MindyGK

We have already seen that putting yourself in the right state and the right environment can create more and better thoughts. Focusing on caring and sharing develops these traits into strong habits which become part of your nature. Now, imagine if you could act from this powerful place all the time. You can! It is your true nature, the one you had before your head (and possibly heart) became clouded and mistrustful. It is your natural state, where you will feel at peace because you know you are being true to your purpose.

Remember, you are not doing this work for self-serving reasons. You are part of an intricate value chain and ecosystem that contains other people, and their feelings, hopes and dreams. Not everyone will respond to your message, or possibly not immediately. Everyone is going through their own challenges, which is the reason why you set out to help them in the first place. But maybe the time isn't right for them to absorb what you are trying to share. Maybe they are not ready to hear it… yet.

This might help you see what I mean. My favorite flowers are lilies. I really love their scent and the look of a stem full of blooms. However, the lilies I like best are the ones where the blooms are all at different stages of opening. Some are just open a crack, others on the same stem are more open, and other flowers on the stem are wide open, gloriously stretching out their petals (and threatening to stain my windowsill with that yellow powder!). Looking at the stem with the blooms at various stages reminds me of the infinite variety in people, personalities, and stages of growth. I put more water into the vase and each of the blooms uses that water to move to the next stage of its development. I don't control that, I just try to nourish the entire planet. I mean, plant.

Are you doing what you can do nourish the plants in your life? Or the planet? Because there are definitely people crying out for what you can give them. As we near the end of my message to you, and send you off to do your best thinking as a thoughtful leader, I'd just like to share with you one of the most popular Thought Bites, originally from *24 Carat BOLD*:

> **Thought Bite:** Those who nourish, flourish @MindyGK

Your clients, your staff and your colleagues need you to be a big thinker. The world needs you to have your best thoughts and your biggest thoughts. If you were to operate from that perspective, one where you are working for a higher purpose, would you be inclined to do whatever was needed to serve? I believe you would, because you are a good person and a committed leader. Yes, it can be hard to find the time, or make the extra effort, but I hope by now you believe it is worth it. Even taking a small step to be a more thoughtful leader is worth it. You have actually taken that step by reading to the end of this book. I love you and I thank you.

> **Thought Bite:** The world needs you to have your best thoughts and your biggest thoughts @MindyGK

Conclusion

I hope I have inspired you to think about your own leadership and if or how it could be more thoughtful. In both senses of the word.

There is no right or wrong here. Although I have noticed my most successful clients operating from a positive state, making time to think and be creative, and generally thinking of others as well as themselves.

Even if you feel you have a long way to go with this stuff, simply being aware of it and interested in improving yourself as a person and a leader is already a huge step. Intention is more valuable than people normally give it credit for. If you have a positive intention for your life, your work and your thoughtful leadership, that is a very good start!

Reflection is not something we are used to doing anymore. Carve out time to reflect on the important issues and opportunities in your life and business, and you will soon see that you are striding ahead of the pack. Not with the goal of being the top dog, remember, but being the top leader of your people.

Caring is optional, but hopefully by now you have seen it doesn't require much more effort to approach life from a caring and sharing perspective. When you get feedback from your actions, you will be inclined to do more of it. And it helps people see the best in you, which will encourage them to follow you and believe in you.

As I mentioned at the beginning, I purposely kept this book as short as possible, while still covering all the key points. If you are seeking more in-depth information and discussion on any of these points, simply get in touch with me. I'm very easy to find online, and happy to speak with people offline – by phone or in person – as I travel around the world sharing these ideas. I look forward to hearing from you, and helping you in whatever way I can. Go out there, be bold, be brave, and most of all – be thoughtful!

Connect with me:

My websites:
www.thethoughtfulleader.com
www.mindygk.com
www.bookmidwife.com
www.panomapress.com

LinkedIn:
www.uk.linkedin.com/in/mindy.gibbinsklein

YouTube:
www.youtube.com/user/bookmidwife

Twitter:
www.twitter.com/bookmidwife

Facebook:
www.facebook.com/mindy.gibbinsklein

Phone numbers (what a novel idea!):
UK +44 (0) 8345 003 8848 or USA +1 (855) 883-1202